JANICE MCDONALD

FEAR

LESS

Girls with Dreams, Women with Vision

● ● **PAGE TWO** BOOKS

Cataloguing in publication information is available from Library and Archives Canada.

ISBN 978-1-989603-03-1 (hardcover)
ISBN 978-1-989603-04-8 (ebook)

Page Two
www.pagetwo.com

Edited by Melissa Edwards
Cover and interior design by Taysia Louie
Printed and bound in Canada by Friesens
Distributed in Canada by Raincoast Books
Distributed in the US and internationally by
Publishers Group West, a division of Ingram

PHOTO CREDITS
p. 21: Katherine Holland
p. 25: Michelle Valberg
p. 34: Courtesy of Couvrette/Ottawa
p. 36: Robert Simons
p. 60: South China Morning Post

All uncredited photos courtesy the contributing women

20 21 22 23 24   5 4 3 2 1

thefearless.shop

For S, A, V, B, and M . . . my CareBears.

Contents

Celebrating the Fearless Girl within Us All

WHEN I THINK of a fearless woman, various things come to mind. Perhaps she has tales of remarkable exploits, has overcome incredible challenges, or has soared to great heights. Her courage may be shown in other ways, too: small and quiet feats of "Wonder Womanean" (as opposed to Herculean) strength, displayed simply by putting one foot in front of the other. This book has long been a dream of mine, and I brought it into the world as a way to shine a spotlight on the experiences of diverse women as they move from being the fearless girl they once were to the fabulous women they now are.

Fearless is a collaborative effort, created to share authentic women's stories on how we've evolved from our earliest days. Together, those featured in these pages are an inspiring collection of different accomplishments, backgrounds, and experiences. Some are names you know well, and others you're likely learning about for the first time. Each stands in her full power, shining a light for others to follow.

I've kept a picture of my ten-year-old self close at hand for many years. It has moved from office to office as my place of work has changed, but its location at the top right-hand corner of my desk has largely stayed the same. The picture is like a North Star for me. When I look at that girl, I see someone who is determined, certain, and fearless. The original version of my true self. And she comes from a long line of formidable women.

Who we are can sometimes get lost along the way as life bumps us and shoves us into different roles and expectations. Societal pressures of what a woman is or should be get piled on top and, suddenly, many of us find ourselves a long way from the girl we once were.

The picture is like a North Star for me. When I look at that girl, I see someone who is determined, certain, and fearless.

Over the course of my career, I've been invited to address larger and larger audiences around the world, and I often share my Fearless Photo as both homework and inspiration for others—I tell them to find a picture of their younger self, and to remember the fearlessness they once possessed. Each time I do this, I come to realize more and more that many women have indeed lost touch with their younger selves. Countless times, women have shared with me how invaluable they found it to dig up that box of old photos, sort through them, and reconnect with who they used to be. Once those Fearless Photos are found, many, like me, begin keeping the image of that girl close by.

The goal of this book is for all of us to tell our stories and share the twists and turns of the lives we have lived. These are women who have forged forward because stopping or giving up was never an option. Some of the stories are heart-breakingly hard to read. Others will lift you up. All will inspire you. I invited many women to take part in this book, and not all said yes. Most of those who declined had a variety of reasons that were easy to accept. But some felt that their stories weren't important enough to be told. I struggled with those responses, as I knew they had experiences to share that would mean a lot to other women. So I nudged them, and sometimes nudged them again. And, thankfully, many did send in their stories, each as compelling and inspiring as I knew they would be.

I am grateful to every woman who took the time to contemplate their journey, and to send it in to be included in this book. I hope you will be as moved and inspired by these stories as I have been.

JANICE MCDONALD

DARE

"THE WOMAN WHO DOES
NOT REQUIRE VALIDATION
FROM ANYONE IS THE
MOST FEARED INDIVIDUAL
ON THE PLANET."

Mohadesa Najumi

Moving Toward Courage

MORE THAN TWELVE hundred years have passed since the Sufi poet Rumi was alive, and yet his writings continue to inspire. I love this line in particular: "Move within, but don't move the way fear makes you move." It's so beautiful. To me, it tells us to choose differently from how fear makes us want to move. Fear is powerful. It can paralyze you when it's left to run wild in your mind. It whispers *you can't, you shouldn't, don't.* It grows in strength every day it stands untested and unquestioned.

Entrepreneurs are, by their very nature, comfortable taking risks. They test and question their fears as they take their ideas out into the marketplace. I have been an entrepreneur since 1991, when I launched my first company. Back then, working on my first master's degree and starting a business at the same time somehow seemed like a manageable combination of activities. I was fearless. My partner and I had no start-up community to turn to, but it didn't matter. No one started up! That term didn't even exist. One day in July we turned on the "open" sign, and our idea for a warehouse retail music store became reality.

In my early twenties, there was simplicity in opening a business. Was it because I knew so little of what could go wrong? Or because my confidence was so strong? Either way, I was unstoppable. Some days I wish I could go back and retrieve that fearlessness. I want to take a bottle of it off the shelf and drink it down. It seemed so easy to be bold and to push myself and my team to take on the industry and innovate in big and small ways. And it worked.

The 1990s were an exciting time of change in the music industry, with compact discs replacing cassettes and a feeling of endless possibilities driving my daily activities. We pushed boundaries and had fun along the way. We created a strong brand that won industry awards and loyal customers. When I look back, I'm amazed at all we achieved. I'm still bold, but, somehow, it's more nuanced. I understand that things can get complicated in business and in life. The complications make me thirsty for boldness, and sometimes it seems to be in short supply.

But not here. All of the women who tell their stories in this chapter have an unquenchable desire to, as Rumi states, move despite the fear, and to move toward courage.

JANICE

KATIE TELFORD

IT'S OFTEN ASSUMED that people become more cautious with age and are held back by societal conventions that are learned over time. Yet, for me, what connects this photo with the next is a commitment to remaining fearless while serving within Canada's democratic institutions. Some of my friends say I am more fearless today than I have ever been as I work to create a unique space in the political sphere and in civic discourse, and to find ways to share this space with others—particularly with more women.

When I was twelve, I walked on the floor of the Ontario Legislature as a page—the youngest in my group! I delivered notes between ministers and tabled the budget on the desks of members of provincial parliament. It was a quiet role, but an essential one. A role that even let me take time out from school. Being in that chamber—living the traditions of the parliamentary system and witnessing the politics of the day—was a privilege and an experience that left a lasting impression on me.

I dove into the world of partisan politics in my twenties. To advance in that arena, I had to find and know my voice and cultivate the values I would fight for. I had to make space for myself, and for other women. I built networks and relationships that challenged and supported me, and encouraged opportunities. I had to say yes to new things. I had to take risks. I had to acquire the ability to manage through extreme pressure and to accept public scrutiny.

I had to say yes to new things. I had to take risks. I had to acquire the ability to manage through extreme pressure and to accept public scrutiny.

None of this growth happened without overcoming some failure. But, thanks to that early personal drive (and push by my parents—my first backers!), I was able to pick myself up from campaigns that were lost, policy attempts that were unsuccessful, and bad-news days. I had the courage to walk into new places, to question, and to be steadfast in my respect for our democratic institutions.

I now hold one of the most senior positions in the highest political office in the country. As chief of staff, I not only observe and learn, I also speak up and advise the prime minister of Canada. It is a role that demands fearlessness—and a role that I hope fearless women will continue to occupy.

KATIE TELFORD is the chief of staff to Prime Minister of Canada Justin Trudeau. She previously served as the national campaign co-chair and national campaign director for the Liberal Party of Canada's successful 2015 federal election campaign. Over the course of her career, Telford has provided senior counsel on a wide range of federal and provincial issues to non-profit organizations, the private and public sectors, and political parties.

LESLIE WOO

IN LIFE, SOMETIMES we get a big *push* that tests our bravery and resilience. Over the span of my life, I have come to embrace this unknown.

This first picture was taken in the 1970s in Bloomington, Indiana, when I was eight years old. I spent six months away from my parents, living with my aunt and her family in the graduate student housing at Indiana University. In the background you can see the tower where we lived.

The photo was taken in the playground. I am sporting a short "Mary Quant" bob haircut, bell-bottoms, and a buttoned-up floral shirt. Not so unordinary. But the story behind the picture is not just that this young girl was from the small Caribbean island of Trinidad, but also that she attended the state's first alternative school, she was one of the first in the test group for fluoride, she learned how to make the quintessential peanut butter and jelly sandwiches on her own, cared for younger cousins, and had recently experienced Halloween for the first time.

This trip was my first memory of true independence. It was here that my uncle taught me how to be scrappy against bullies. I had grown up in a country of visible diversity, where everyone mixed together. I didn't even recognize that I was different-looking at that age. Maybe that explains my downward look in the photo. My memory of that time is very mixed, as I was homesick, while excited at the idea of making new friends. I am grateful to my uncle, an amateur photographer, for recording most of my time there. Bloomington was a *push* into my ongoing streak of independence. Upon my return to Trinidad, I found a voice that I didn't know I had. In fact, I distinctly remember my mum turning to me in the back seat of our car, shortly after my return, and exclaiming that my back-talk was clearly a bad trait that I had picked up from the Americans.

Today, I use that confident independence toward impact. The bright light of changing things for the better both blinds me and draws me in. My second photo, a recent one, is the inverse of the first. I am facing bright lights, but at the same time speaking into the darkness. It was taken in Sydney, Australia, where, as the invited keynote for a biannual transit industry conference, I am talking to hundreds about the future of mobility and how it will reshape cities. I am looking up and outward. When I look at this photo, I feel strong. Fearlessness is probably linked to a certain love of the unknown—the darkness. If each of us knew ahead of time the challenges that life held for us, it's possible we might all curl up in a ball and never move.

These two pictures exaggerate the fearlessness in me, with which I try to make an impact in my small way. Early on, good people pushed me into uncharted waters—they were confident I could stay afloat—and the more that happens to me, the more adaptive and resilient I become. Today, I fearlessly and deliberately seek the uncharted in my goal to be part of building better cities.

LESLIE WOO is an architect, urban planner, and land developer. Woo has been named one of Canada's 2017 Top 100 Most Powerful Women and a 2015 Women's Infrastructure Network Outstanding Leader; currently, she uses her blog (shebuilds cities.org) to showcase women city builders—a legacy project following her Fellowship with the International Women's Forum.

ANNA LAMBERT

THIS IS THE eleven-year-old version of me, starring in a production of *Annie*. For many, being on stage creates—rather than relieves—a sense of fear. But during a particularly anxious time in my childhood, acting became my outlet. It sounds counterintuitive, but I found a place of comfort on the stage, performing for others. Acting in a lead role was my first real foray into being centre stage. It was a way for me to "try on" being confident and smart, by being someone else.

This photo reminds me of how confident I felt on stage, being Annie.

I stopped acting after high school and jumped head-first into university—I landed my first "real" job at a forty-person start-up in Ottawa called Shopify. Over the next seven years I would go on to learn and stretch myself more than I could ever imagine. I started out as an intern, and worked my way up to become the director of a global talent acquisition team in a very short period of time. My team and I have helped the company grow from 150 people to well over 4,000 amazing employees.

In my role, I often find myself speaking publicly at conferences and events—but now, I'm not pretending to be someone else. In March 2019, I did a TEDx talk. It took a lot of effort to prepare, but once I landed on stage, I felt a sense of calm and presence. I was blown away—people were there to hear what I had to say.

This second photo reminds me of how confident I now feel on stage, being Anna.

———————

As a director of talent acquisition at Shopify, ANNA LAMBERT leads a team of more than one hundred people across seven locations globally. Over the last seven years, she has contributed to Shopify's growth by designing high-impact teams who serve the company's global merchant base. Lambert was named one of the *Ottawa Business Journal*'s top 40 under 40 in 2018.

KRISTINE MCGINN

'M A BELLEVILLE girl. The product of a small Ontario town, a hard-working, middle-class family, and all that this means: traditional values and even more traditional gender-role expectations. I was the third of three girls, born before the only boy, and pictures of me are scarce—though there is this early one of me with my sisters, the meat in a girly-girl sandwich.

In spite of efforts to mould me in the "pink or blue" image of the early-1970s status quo, it always seemed to me that what the boys were doing was much more interesting. In grade 6, I announced that I wanted to play lacrosse, one of the roughest sports out there. The answer was no. I persisted. They relented. As the only girl in the league, I was not permitted to get ready with my teammates in the changeroom. I was relegated to a public washroom, where I strained to hear a muffled version of the pre-game huddle and hype. I was literally on the outside, looking in, and I had my doubts. I didn't have the brawn, so I earned the respect of my teammates by being fast on my feet and strategic. Although I think he had his eyes closed most of the time, my dad never missed a game. The whole experience taught me a valuable lesson: if you want a level playing field, sometimes you have to level it yourself. If there is no path, make one.

I was proud to choose a traditional career in nursing (and I think it was a tremendous relief to my parents), but I chafed at the inefficiencies that I observed daily, and longed to make improvements to the care delivery

The whole experience taught me a valuable lesson: if you want a level playing field, sometimes you have to level it yourself. If there is no path, make one.

system. Changing a bureaucratic beast on my own was a near impossibility, so I started a healthcare consulting company for patients recovering from physical and psychological disabilities.

I had no business degree and no entrepreneurial role models to look to. Once again, I was that little girl on the lacrosse team. But, just like that little girl, I ended up a high scorer. I am proud of the successful company I created, and the meaningful difference my team and I made in the lives of others. I learned again that having passion for what you are doing is the single most important driver to success.

A few years ago, a friend asked me to join her on a 110-mile kayak adventure in the Baja with an elite group of paddlers. It would be ten days on the ocean, sleeping in tents in the desert and relying on ourselves and each other for survival. There are a million reasons I should have said no. I had kayaked only a few times, had never pitched a tent alone, and the thought of being off the grid and relying on strangers terrified me. In spite of it all, I went along blindly—literally. I had forgotten my contacts.

Full disclosure: I cried for the first three days. But on the fourth, I decided to embrace the experience, and to rely on my skills and those of my team.

Looking at a photo of me from the last day of the trip, I see the brave, bold, strong girl that I was, and the woman I am.

Today, I am co-owner of a fast-growing home healthcare company—one that my business partner and I have built from our passion to challenge the status quo, and that has a culture we are proud of. The lessons I learned in life have become a solid foundation for a can-do attitude that celebrates the uniqueness of each individual I encounter.

KRISTINE MCGINN is an entrepreneur and COO/co-owner of Assurance Health Care, a leading provider of innovative, quality homecare for seniors. She brings world-class expertise to this role, built on many years dedicated to patient care as a nurse, professor, business owner, and volunteer. McGinn is also chair of the DIFD, which works to change the dialogue around youth mental health.

SANGITA PATEL

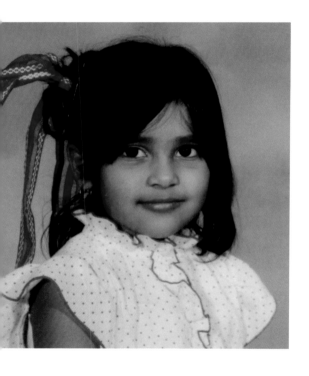

I **WAS BORN ON** January 2, 1979, as the third child in the family. My parents had come to Canada not long before—my dad had left my mom in India while she was pregnant with my brother to start a better life for his family in North America. I can't even imagine the struggles they went through to make a life in their new country, leaving behind everything they knew in India. I saw firsthand what they had to go through to survive, and watching them taught me the value of hard work. What parents would do for their kids.

I've had the privilege of being raised in a country where I knew I had opportunities. That little kid in the photo with ribbons in her hair has always been ambitious. She was always trying something new, never letting her skin colour, her culture, or her beliefs get in the way. She was full of energy, happy, and never, ever gave up.

I always ask one question: Why not? And that question has led me along so many different paths, from being an electrical engineer to now appearing on television, covering entertainment and hosting an HGTV show.

I'm forty now, and truly blessed—with incredible kids, husband, my family, a career I love, and a passion for life. That little girl with the ribbons is still me. Live life to the fullest.

SANGITA PATEL is currently the host of HGTV's *Home to Win* and an on-air personality with *Entertainment Tonight Canada*. She has a major passion for fitness, food (usually healthy), and having those "real" conversations. She is happily married and the proud mother of Ava and Shyla, who keep her on her toes and are definitely the best gifts in her life.

CATHERINE LANDRY

CATHERINE is very *bossy and likes to make sure everything is done her way, and she gets discouraged when things are not going the way she planned.* She is kind-hearted and always helps her classmates, and she sticks up for the children who are feeling left out, managing to include everyone in her world. Catherine has a propensity to learn tasks very quickly, but needs to focus. She enjoys her snack and likes to skip naptime, opting to read or colour instead. Her colouring skills are excellent, but she chooses to stay outside the lines and actually re-draws the colouring book to suit herself. If she would focus more on the task at hand, that would be perfect. Catherine is also always barefoot. She's a pleasure to have in class.

I GREW UP in Lagos, Nigeria, and this is me with my wonderful nannies. I believe the one thing we all need to realize is that, as business women, our destiny was created a very long time ago—and the person we were as a child is the person who is now our core. Go back and review who you were at three,

and you will find that this is the person you are now, in business. That person is *not* an inner child; they are an inner entrepreneur. You were born with that spirit invested deep in your DNA. Honour it and rise up to greet it every day, because it is *you*, and it is who you were destined to be. Everything you are when you are three, that is who you will always be.

———————

CATHERINE LANDRY is the CEO of Call Betty! Marketing and the founder of sheshopslocal.ca and Ladies Who Lunch Ottawa.

JENNIFER STEWART

WHEN I WAS young, I was shy when I wasn't with my family. I wanted to please all my teachers, and thought very carefully about what words would come out of my mouth before I ever spoke.

Sometime around the age that this first picture was taken, an announcement came on the school PA system. A ring with a "green jewel" had been found, and the owner was to come to the office. The ring was mine, and it was my coveted little treasure from a rink vending machine. But just the thought of standing up in class and going to claim my ring instilled me with overwhelming fear.

It wasn't until university that I truly found my voice, and the liberty of embracing my talents and shedding the cloak of self-doubt. I was taking journalism at Carleton University and felt empowered with the sense of ownership that comes with editing the local school paper and telling the stories of those around me. I also learned to push people for answers, and not always to be the source of someone else's happiness.

The photo on the next page was taken five years ago, and marks five years as an entrepreneur. At the time, I had a one-year-old at home, and was pregnant with my second child. I had found an extreme amount of purpose

in running a business, learning to negotiate, and landing a deal. As a woman within a sector of men, I thrived on proving people wrong and nurturing a growing business.

If I could tell that shy girl anything, I would say, "You did everything right." We have an emphasis on telling women that they need to find their voice and speak up immediately. But growth takes time, and it takes experience. We need to have patience with ourselves, but take the path that fuels our drive. It makes the journey all that much more rewarding.

As president and founder of Syntax Strategic, JENNIFER STEWART is a leader in the strategic communications sector, and a regular commentator for CTV. She has been named one of the Top 25 People in the Capital by *Ottawa Life* and a Top Forty Under 40 by the *Ottawa Business Journal*, and was a finalist for Ottawa's Female Entrepreneur of the Year award.

SANDRA HENDERSON

AS A YOUNG lady, I was confident—shaped by good academics and a good natural athletic ability, both of which helped me "hang with the boys." I was able to skate and play hockey, but I also excelled in math and sciences. When you can do things like that, you end up being named as a tomboy, and somehow that makes striving for new heights even easier.

The picture you'll see on the next page was actually a very rare feminine photo for me. I remember the day—wearing clothes that did not suit my normal way of dressing, hair being done, and being asked to sit through a photo shoot with my family.

Would I describe myself as fearless back then? Probably not. But I did acknowledge that things were not always fair, and I did work a little harder to ensure I was at the top of the class or always invited back for the next pick-up hockey game in our neighbourhood.

As I was growing up, my family was transferred quite a few times for my father's career. Moving to new communities, meeting new friends, joining new sports teams, and figuring out a new school system gave me skills: flexibility, adaptability, and courage. I had to learn to take on new tasks, and not to be afraid when some came with risks.

Because of all this, I've been fortunate to believe that you can have it all: a strong connection with family, lots of great friends, and a successful career. People ask me sometimes if I have the balance right. All I can say is that there is always a give and take. I tried to never miss important sports and

I have been so fortunate to have a wonderful role model in my mom, who always told me: "You can, and you should."

school events for my children, but at the same time I wasn't always home every night for dinner.

One of the key factors in my career has been the ability to be mobile and open to all possibilities. We have moved ten times across North America. Each time, I took the risk that the move would both be beneficial for my career and would work for our family. Having the courage to take on new roles, sometimes completely out of my comfort zone, led to many new doors, and I gained substantial new experiences.

Earlier on in my career, I didn't really focus on the fact that I was a female executive in a male-dominated environment. I think that came from my younger days, when I mainly in classes with boys, or playing sports with boys. There were certainly some barriers, but I believe courage let me jump into the mix and never hold back.

I have been so fortunate to have a wonderful role model in my mom, who always told me: "You can, and you should." She was the one who encouraged me in math and sciences, and always put me into every sport possible. I believe that I have passed that along to my daughter—encouraging her to take risks, and to be courageous.

———

SANDRA HENDERSON is chief operating officer for BMO Private Wealth, responsible for leading the planning and implementation of product and service strategies for the business. Henderson serves on the boards of the International Women's Forum Canada and the Women in a Supported Environment Leadership Advisory Board.

CONN

ECT

"WE LIVE BY EACH OTHER
AND FOR EACH OTHER...
TOGETHER WE
CAN DO SO MUCH."

Helen Keller

Our Networks
Are Powerful

MY VINTAGE PINBALL machine—called Pin-Bot—is a favourite in my family when we're looking for a little friendly competition. The top score on the board is a coveted position. The pleasure of tapping in your initials, where they remain until usurped, is a point of pride for all of us. This is unproven, but one overly competitive family member may have even unplugged the machine to reset the top score. For our next family gathering, we've come up with a new twist to the challenge: we're going to apply a round robin approach—like with tennis—where names will be matched for play and only the winner will move on. There's a lot of excitement about it in our family group chat and we'll make an evening of it soon enough.

I may be a pinball wizard, but I equally love board games. If Connect Four comes out when we're on holiday, I can easily get lost playing for hours. It's been known under that name since 1974, but it's actually a centuries-old game. Legend has it that Captain James Cook played it with his fellow officers on his long voyages, which is why it's also known as "Captain's Mistress." Regardless of the name, the goal of this two-player game is always to form a single line of four coloured discs. The first player to do so wins the game. Simple, and yet fun enough to while away the hours.

Networking is like Connect Four. You can easily be out every night meeting new people. When done right, networking is all about aligning connections to win—and winning can be in the form of new business, introductions, information, and so many other opportunities. When created, nurtured, and used, networks are powerful tools. I teach a five-day Advancing Women Leaders program along with my colleague, Clare, and in one exercise, we have the women leaders map their networks. They take the time to see where their networks are robust and where they need to bolster certain groups. It's a helpful exercise, and it shows the value of having a strong and connected network.

The women featured here sometimes rely on the support of others, and sometimes offer their support in return—but all are connectors who bring people together. They look for ways to introduce others, and strive to strengthen their own relationships and expand their networks. These are women who truly understand the power of a linked group of people.

JANICE

VICKI HEYMAN

I AM A FIRSTBORN child with two younger siblings: my sister, Gwen, and my brother, Spencer. With our parents, Sharon and Bob, we lived in a small river town of thirty thousand people in eastern Kentucky, where our family owned and operated an apparel shop—the Star Store. My parents worked in the store six days a week, and I regularly helped out as well. I wrapped gifts during the holidays, helped customers in the teen department put together just the right outfits, assisted in the bridal department; you name it, I did it.

The Star Store allowed our family to engage with our community, and from an early age I learned how to listen to peoples' stories and relate to them. I loved interacting with everyone, and age or other differences were never intimidating. I can remember as a first grader being assigned the role of narrator in a multi-grade school play. I was unfazed by what was perhaps my first "leadership role," in a cast with children five years older than I was. As my mother told it, she knew then that I would be able to hold my own in the world, and create meaningful relationships with people from all walks of life.

My parents emphasized good manners, and I grew up steeped in the importance of human connection. Throughout my childhood, I never had one "thing"; I wasn't a math whiz or a track star, but—woven through every aspect of my life—I had a consistent passion for understanding and connecting with people. All of this has informed my personal definition of "home"; home is not a physical structure, it's a web of people, shared bonds, and

relationships. It's not a place, it's a feeling—a grounded feeling of warmth and security that empowers us to forge our own paths and create our own communities out in the world.

All my life I have tried to practice this belief. Every time I move, or even visit a new place, my goal is to understand and connect to the people in the community. I seek out their stories just like I did as a child at the Star Store. Through this, I gain rich relationships, a deeper understanding of our world, and a better sense of my place in it.

The picture above shows me as a five-year-old standing in front of my family home. The first picture was taken fifty years later, as an adult, after I had moved one year earlier from Chicago to Lornado, the US ambassador's residence in Ottawa. When my husband, Bruce, and I arrived at Lornado,

As my mother told it, she knew then that I would be able to hold my own in the world, and create meaningful relationships with people from all walks of life.

we wanted it to be the "front door" of the US to Canadians. Before we even had our furniture moved in, we opened the house to a group of authors and civic leaders and, later that week, to the Ottawa Press Corps. Throughout our three years in Ottawa, we welcomed over ten thousand people to Lornado, whether on the front lawn for the 4th of July or inside for intimate salons and dinner parties, where we discussed art, culture, and issues of the day.

Lornado became my grown-up version of the Star Store—a place for community members to gather, share their stories, and unite over their similarities and differences. In many ways, the woman in the later photo is worlds away from that little girl in eastern Kentucky. But in both photos, I am home. Each depicts a person who, with quiet confidence, has reached out to her community, forged relationships, and put down roots to create a home for herself.

VICKI HEYMAN has taken an active leadership role as an American cultural representative. She has served as co-chair of the Illinois Finance Committee for the Obama for America campaign, and was an active member of the Obama for America National Finance Committees. Extremely dedicated to worthy causes, Heyman currently leads the Vicki and Bruce Heyman Charitable Trust.

MARIKA BUZZA

GROWING UP, I spent most of my time wondering if I should be somewhere else.

With parents from polar opposite sides of the world, I was always trying to find the place where I belonged. Not here or there, but both. Or rather, somewhere in between. See how these eyes look like I've been caught somewhere I shouldn't be?

In our home, there were two cultures dancing with and around one another. There were conversations happening in different languages across and over each other at the dinner table. We played Japanese card games and watched Canadian hockey on television. We spent summers at firework festivals in Kōfu, and winters making snowmen in Ottawa. Yet, in our home, which felt like a small pond, my mom and dad created a world in which these cultures shared space, coexisting in unity.

Since then, the pond has grown to become oceans. While time doesn't make a girl love a floral dress any less, it will offer her many experiences she couldn't have even dreamt of. My dad tells me, *opportunity dances with those who are already on the dance floor*. In retrospect, I see how so many of the opportunities I've been given were because of something that came before it. I got to do this, because of that. And looking forward, I'll get to do that because of this.

The woman who created this book gifted me advice that I carry with me every day. She took me on, big eyed with more questions than even I could keep up with. My knees would buckle every time I got up to speak. That's

My dad tells me, "opportunity dances with those who are already on the dance floor."

when she said, *walk into the room like you've been there before.* These words were too big for me to appreciate in that moment, but I've started to understand what she meant. Now, I walk into rooms with confidence: *I've done this before.* Because I have. In some way, all of the opportunities and experiences that I've gathered up to now have led me to be in this room. I walk in with my head held high, carrying all my learnings with me.

My parents named me Marika. In Japanese culture, it's a tradition that your grandparents give symbolic characters to your name. My grandparents chose 万里香 [ma-ri-ka], which my grandmother writes in the most beautiful calligraphy each year on the birthday card she sends. The characters tell a story of villages that cross thousands of miles, all while carrying the same scent of love. My mom tells me that I am that scent. That despite the distance and differences, I will find my place in both worlds, and in each room, carrying my scent of love.

I don't wonder so much if I should be somewhere else anymore. I'm no longer in search of a place to call mine. At this moment, I'm proud to be exactly where I'm meant to be. I am the place I've been looking for.

I'll see you on the dance floor, girl.

MARIKA BUZZA is a lover of tea cups and handwritten notes. After completing her studies, she worked with the Beacon Agency to travel across Canada, interviewing women entrepreneurs on their stories of innovation. She currently works at Shopify, helping make commerce better for everyone.

CLAUDINE PILON

I HAVE SO MANY pictures, tons of pictures, almost all of them were taken when I was with the people I love: friends, family, co-workers. I am rarely shown alone, and all are filled with terrific memories. And I guess that describes me best: A people person. A team player.

In this first one, I'm sitting on a chair at my summer cottage in the Eastern Townships (about an hour southeast of Montreal). I love this picture. I'm in my late thirties. It's September, my favourite month. It's my birthday. Just outside of the frame are my friends and family, who came to celebrate this important moment with me and my husband. Why was it so special? Not so long after this photo was taken, my husband and I moved out west—the boldest move we had ever done. We left family and friends, a good home, secure jobs. In one seventy-two-hour period, we had decided what would change our future forever.

No regrets, though. We spent three years in Alberta and British Columbia, discovering our great country, meeting new people, and forging great relationships. Five years later, we came back to our home province to be there for our aging parents. Again, no regrets. It created other terrific opportunities, like working at BDC today.

Can I really describe myself as fearless? Maybe.

I discovered quickly that I am my strongest when I am inspired by others and what they do. I've never been afraid to say no, if it's for the right reason. I'm certainly never afraid to support and promote people and their great work. I've never been afraid to get out of my comfort zone and jump into the unknown.

And I am very content with the decisions I have made, both in my professional life and in my personal life.

If all of this means being fearless, then yes, I guess I am.

CLAUDINE PILON is senior advisor, external communications, at the Business Development Bank of Canada (BDC). As the integrated marketing and communication lead for the bank's Women Entrepreneurs strategy, her greatest motivation is helping others achieve success, promoting entrepreneurships, and communicating the passion, purpose, and perseverance of women entrepreneurs BDC proudly serves.

HENRIETTA SOUTHAM

BELIEVE MY STRENGTH has always resided in a body of water to which I have been tethered my entire life. We are born from the water of our mothers and, as far as it goes for me, I will be laid to rest in the lake that has been in my family for over a century. The very water in which my brother and I dispersed our mother's ashes, two days ago from the time I write this.

Belonging to a place, no matter its quality, is in and of itself a power to reckon with. You would expect that, for someone with deep ancestral roots in one country, I would feel grounded. As it turns out, I was born into turmoil, which went hand-in-hand with moving from one continent to another, one country to another, one city to another. Living in London, Paris, Toronto, New York, and Miami, with spring and winters in Norway and Italy, Barbados or the south of France... all times and places as iconic as they were idyllic. Except we were nomads. We never owned anything but fleeting memories of the sun, snow, sounds, and smells of each countryside and cityscape.

Throughout, there was only one constant: summers at The Lake. Here, too, family upheaval followed. I remember vividly the last night my father lived on the island he fought for in the Second World War. After a terrible row with my half-brother, his eldest son, he woke me from my deep university-student sleep in the boathouse of Bending Birches, the island my mother had brought me to at two weeks old, and told me to get into the blue boat. And off we went, never to step back on the island ever again, as dweller or owner. It now belonged to the children of my father's first wife. My father rebuilt a

Belonging to a place, no matter its quality, is in and of itself a power to reckon with.

summer home on an island not far over that he called "All Is Best." Here, I spent snippets of each summer as a young wife and mother to my two boys. The island belonged to my father's third and last wife, and so, upon both their passing, the land passed to my step-sister.

For many years I did not understand why and where I belonged on this lake. Until I understood that I belonged to the *water* of the lake. The smells of warm pine needles and fish scales, green algae and cedar waft upward come sun or storm upon each crossing, saying "hello and welcome back" or "goodbye and see you soon." But the one unspoken promise and profoundly teachable feeling that forever calms and soothes me remains: "I will always be here for you."

These photos were taken during such lake crossings. The first was taken by my mother on the powerful blue boat as we went into town. I see in me an eight-year-old girl who is staring down the difficult years that lie ahead, unwavering and unbowed, pressing solidly into the headwinds she so fully embraces. The second was taken by my own eight-year-old daughter as I crossed back to the sunny island I bought for my children, away from the family fray on the other side of the lake. I see a woman who has liberated herself from her fear of never belonging, of never being loved, or, worse, capable of loving. I see a daughter undefeated. I see a mother worthy of extraordinary children. I see a woman who has conquered what matters most.

HENRIETTA SOUTHAM is founder and principal at HS Design, a full-service design firm based in Ottawa, and works internationally as a designer, writer, and photographer. Southam sits on the board of directors of the Council for Canadian American Relations and is a founding director of the National Health and Fitness Institute in Canada.

TISHA RATTOS

I AM A FIRST-GENERATION Canadian and an only child. Our heritage is from Goa, India, but my parents were born in Kenya and immigrated to Toronto in the 1970s, and they worked hard to make a great life for us. Growing up in the suburbs of Toronto wasn't always easy; it came with cultural biases that sometimes affected my introversion and confidence. But every goal I wanted to reach, every ladder I wanted to climb, was always encouraged, and I learned dedication and courage of conviction.

My most vivid early lesson came when I was thirteen, when a friend asked me to join her soccer league. To the joy of my parents, who were exceptional athletes, I gave it a try. That first season was dismal, and it was evident that I had no skills. But the following season, I was one of the top players. So how did this happen?

It happened because of four things:

- My coach continually motivated and taught me.
- My friend and teammates always encouraged me.
- My parents saw my desire to achieve more, and they trained me.
- And I made a commitment to be better.

I was learning what it meant to help people succeed; I was learning about teamwork, grit, and breaking down biases. I was building self-confidence, and staying true to my authentic self and the values I continue to hold today.

My journey has not been without moments of adversity, both personally and professionally. What has gotten me through has been family, friends, colleagues, leaders, and now my Judy team, whom I continue to learn from. This has all kept me moving forward, and now I can say I am more confident as a person.

Today, I am an executive who has been able to generate robust long-term growth and value by developing business-level strategies. But when I look back, my proudest achievement has been how I exhibit my values to help others succeed, and what they have written to me about being a role model— my humour, integrity, trust, fairness, and striving to do the right thing. It is how I work: "I can, but we will."

I was building self-confidence, and staying true to my authentic self and the values I continue to hold today.

In 2016, encouraged by my friends, I rode the Ride to Conquer Cancer, a 230-kilometre bike trip, in memory of my father, who succumbed to this disease when I was in my twenties. In training for the event (my first time in shoe clips), I fell and injured myself several times, but I continued to practice. The day of the ride was blistering hot, and, exhausted physically and mentally, there were several times when I wanted to quit. Friends, other cyclists, and people on the path kept encouraging, motivating me to keep going. I completed the ride, and a personal feat, in order to give back. It is still one of my biggest accomplishments.

My journey has, and continues to be, about lifelong learning, grit, confidence, and helping others succeed. I continue to value courage of conviction, authenticity, and passion. I am fortunate to have remarkable people, both past and present, who have also supported me in climbing my personal ladder.

An executive in telecommunications, TISHA RATTOS is a strategic influencer and cultural agent for change, who, through transformations, has generated robust long-term growth with shareholder and customer value. Her passions include travelling, food, scotch, and theatre.

JACKIE LANCASTER-MCCARTHY

THIS FIRST PICTURE was taken when I was ten years old and flying with my family to Chicago for my cousin's wedding. I was excited when the plane's engines roared as it accelerated down the runway. It was exhilarating! In the picture, my father is sitting beside me. He was an entrepreneur who came from very humble beginnings. I believe he was adventurous because of his past experiences, which afforded our family many opportunities—opportunities that were a result of his outlook on life, and that had a profound influence on my own life.

The second picture is of me and my daughters this past summer on the Matterhorn in Switzerland. Both of my daughters have flown in an airplane on an annual basis since their first year of life. Most of the trips were in the US or the Caribbean, but when our girls were eleven and nine, we travelled to Rome, Florence, and Venice. When they were thirteen and eleven, we flew to England, Ireland, and

Scotland, and this year we took a train tour in Switzerland. Travelling to some of my "bucket list" locations has given my daughters the opportunity to learn, explore, and experience.

Through my travels and experiences, I have learned that you must "take the bull by the horns" and "step up to the plate" both professionally and personally, which by default results in some individual level of fearlessness. For me, being fearless means taking chances and seizing opportunities. In life, you have to make choices, accept some level of risk and look for opportunities that others might not see. Fear can hold you back, and keep you from reaching your true potential. These are the sentiments I have shared with my daughters in the hopes that they live their best lives, and continue to be the phenomenal women they are meant to be.

————————

JACQUELINE LANCASTER-MCCARTHY has been in the field of aviation for thirty-two years and currently works at NAV CANADA as the commercial relations manager. Lancaster-McCarthy holds a degree in social sciences from the University of Ottawa, a communications certificate from Algonquin College, and is a certified FAA aircraft dispatcher.

ERIN SEEGMILLER

THIS PHOTO EPITOMIZES the summers of my childhood up at the cottage. Whenever I had the chance, I would climb up onto a rock and pretend I was Pocahontas. While the wind swept my hair back, I would sing out over the crashing waves and whistling winds.

There are many photos of me doing this, but this one is significant because, immediately after it was taken, I slipped off the rock and fell into the water. My mother leaped to my rescue, grabbing my flailing arms and lifting me up.

This, of course, would not be the first or last time I'd fall. From school stress to career missteps to relationship blunders, I have and will continue to face challenges and make mistakes.

I've never considered myself to be fearless. There have always been those little voices of self-doubt or hesitation in the back of my mind. But I feel blessed to have had incredible women around me, to look up to and to lift me out of the depths of the darkest water. Their steady words of encouragement have always drowned out those nagging, critical voices in my head.

That support began with my mother on that day when she wiped away my tears and encouraged me to climb back on the rock. Since then, I have had the fortune of being surrounded by female professors, bosses, colleagues,

That support began with my mother on that day when she wiped away my tears and encouraged me to climb back on the rock.

and mentors who have echoed those words—inspiring and enabling me to let my voice be heard over the waves of challenges that life has thrown at me.

I've come to realize that accomplishment is never a matter of being fearless. Fear is inevitable. But I have learned to recognize my fears, and to find the strength to push past them.

Even when I moved far from home, studying in France and working in Australia, I still felt the presence of supportive women lifting me up. I carried their advice and fortitude with me, giving me more and more confidence with each step.

Working in the male-dominated industries of tech and energy, I know there are still mountains women will need to climb. While I rely on the support of the strong women in my life, I vow to provide strength to the women around me, so they too can conquer their fears and let their voices be heard.

———

ERIN SEEGMILLER is part of the Tech4Good Steering Committee and supports tech entrepreneurs at Invest Ottawa, with a special focus on supporting female tech entrepreneurs to grow their start-ups and secure funding. She is passionate about growing Ottawa's tech community.

LAURA DIDYK

I **ALWAYS LOVED SPORTS** and being active. As a kid, whether I was playing volleyball, basketball, ringette, hiking, or just playing outside, I loved the way sport would create camaraderie within my team, and a sense of collaboratively playing to win. Competing in sports helped me gain the courage to pursue and accept career opportunities, even when the challenges took me well outside my comfort zone. I was fortunate to have coaches who taught me, inspired me, and helped me develop the confidence to push to be better—to be the best athlete I could be.

These were more than sports skills; I was learning life skills. This foundation translated easily when I entered the corporate world, as I sought out strong career mentors and coaches. When I joined BDC in 1994, I didn't expect to still be finding new challenges twenty-five years later. With the support of leaders and colleagues, I've taken on progressively more senior positions and even bigger challenges.

I'm so proud of my team and the impact they continue to have with Canadian entrepreneurs. Most recently, in my role working with women business

owners and leaders, I have had the privilege of meeting incredible women in every part of the country. It's amazing knowing that I am surrounded by allies, innovators, trailblazers, mentors, and friends who are all united in one mission: to unleash the full potential of women business owners and leaders.

Since joining the Business Development Bank of Canada (BDC) in 1994, LAURA DIDYK has been passionate about entrepreneurship. She is vice president and national lead, Women Entrepreneurs, at BDC, in which role she leads the bank's national strategy to support Canadian women entrepreneurs and ensures that strategy is integrated across the entire bank.

ANN BORDELON

WHEN I WAS in third grade, I desperately wanted to play on a softball team. I had never played group sports and I was anxious to be a competitor, but mostly I craved to belong to a team. Unfortunately, the youth recreation program on the military base where my family had just moved did not have a softball league for my age group. Refusing to let me be denied my opportunity to play, my mother signed me up for the boys' baseball league.

I vividly remember the day we got our uniforms. I could not wait to get home and put on that Cubs uniform, complete with cap and sock stirrups. I was so excited to be part of a team, even if I was the only girl. I don't think it occurred to me at the time that playing on the boys' team was unusual. I was just thrilled to have a jersey, and anxious to contribute to the team's victories, and to share in the agony of defeat.

From that year on, I was hooked. Sure, I had participated in more individual sports, but I was drawn to the team. I loved the relationships that developed. I loved the group celebrations after a win, and I treasured the sharing of defeat. There is nothing more special than your teammates cheering you on as you step into the batter's box. Those same teammates will

pat you on the back when you let that routine ground ball get by you. I never wanted to let my team down, which was a natural motivator to do my best and to continuously sharpen my skills on the field. I am very grateful for youth sports teams and how they shaped me as person and as a professional.

I couldn't have known when I donned that Cubs baseball uniform for the first time that it would be the first of many, many teams on which I would have the pleasure of serving. I couldn't have known that one of the best teams I would ever be a part of didn't have a uniform at all. There were about twenty of us on the Walmart senior executive finance team. We were about as aligned as a corporate team can be. We developed strategies as a team, shared talent as a team, celebrated wins as a team, and worked together to move the company mission forward as a team.

In July 2010, I joined the Walmart senior finance team and together we rang the closing bell at the NYSE to celebrate the company's 11,000th store opening. And while we may have competed in our individual career progressions, this team was incredibly encouraging and supportive of each other. My peers challenged me to be a better leader and finance professional. They were there to cheer me on, and to offer constructive criticism when I fell short. Just being on that team made me better: I didn't want to let them down, and I wanted to be a leader for my fellow team members. Just as I am grateful for all of the sports teams I represented in my youth, I am immeasurably grateful to my peers on the Walmart finance team, who helped to make me the best leader and finance professional I could be.

ANN BORDELON is a former Walmart finance executive, with roles such as chief audit executive, CFO of Sam's Club, and CFO of Walmart Asia. Bordelon served on the company's first President's Council of Women Leaders and helped launch both the Women's Officer Caucus and Walmart Women in Finance. She also serves on the board of America's Car-Mart (CRMT).

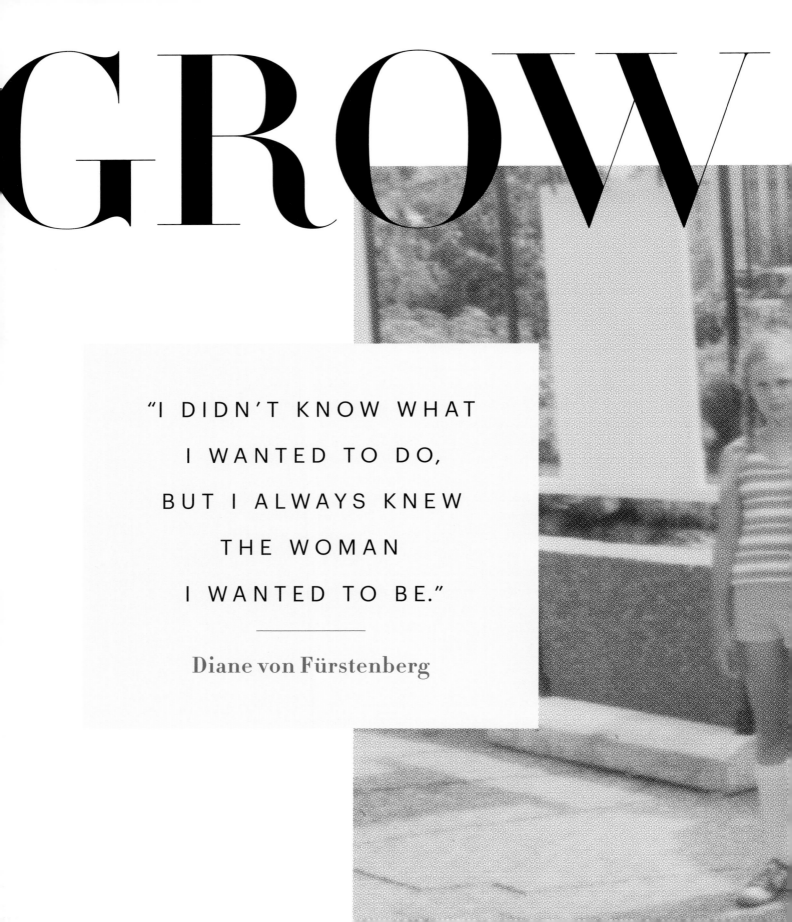

GROW

"I DIDN'T KNOW WHAT
I WANTED TO DO,
BUT I ALWAYS KNEW
THE WOMAN
I WANTED TO BE."

Diane von Fürstenberg

We Never Finish Growing

GROWING UP WITH my sisters, we loved to roam the neighbourhood. Free time was spent outside with the other kids on the street. We managed to keep ourselves very busy with timeless outdoor adventures. One day could involve capturing tadpoles from the ditch, climbing trees, or late-night games of flashlight tag. Our perennial favourite was called Run Around the House. One person was designated "it" and everyone else had to stealthily make it three times around the house without getting caught. I often got covered in mud as I bolted around the corners to get safely to home base. We played that game for hours, summer after summer. When I think back now, I wonder: when did we decide we were too old for these classic games?

These days, my time spent outdoors has me mucking around in the soil as I garden. It's so satisfying, in a different kind of way. It's a quiet and contemplative pursuit. The feeling of cold dirt on my hands as I dig, plant, and weed brings me joy. I imagine new possibilities for myself and for my flower beds with each thrust of the shovel. I've watched with pleasure as a little lilac tree I nurtured became a stately cascade of fragrant flowers. I've probably broken some gardening rules as I've mixed the vegetables among the flowers. Correct placement, ideal soil, and constant attention has resulted in a beautiful bounty of flowers and vegetables, even though I'm not a skilled gardener.

It never quite feels like work when I'm in the garden with a shovel in my hand and my little white dog at my side. The sound of the neighbourhood children playing and laughing makes me smile. Gardening has taught me so many things about life: patience, determination, and creating the right environment for growth, which includes sunlight. Sun is essential for plants to grow. The more sunlight a plant receives, the greater number of flowers it produces.

The women profiled here have stepped into the sunlight, even though it may have been uncomfortable to do so, and even when someone might be slinging mud their way. They continue to inspire with their stories of becoming the strong women they are today, despite the detours they took to get there.

JANICE

JODY THOMAS

THE PHOTO YOU'LL see when you turn the page has been in my parents' home as long as I can remember; the one you see here has sat in my office for two years. Together, they represent a lifetime, one marked by ups and downs, failures and successes, euphoric happiness and profound sadness—not because I am unique, but because that is what a lifetime is.

I am four years old in the second photo. I have fleeting memories of the photo shoot: being proud to wear the new watch my nana had given me; being slightly jealous—as always—of my pretty, well-behaved older sister. I was bursting with life. It's radiating from my face and body. Looking at the photo now, I wonder how my mom ever contained me. I had energy, curiosity, and the confidence of a child who had, even at four, been taught by wonderful, forward-thinking parents that she could do anything and be anything. Chauvinism and sexism were foreign concepts. Self-doubt was not in my lexicon, let alone in my thinking. Life, with all that is good and bad, had yet to happen to me.

I am fifty years old in the photo you see to your left. I am confident in my abilities and love my job as commissioner of the Canadian Coast Guard. I am the adult that four-year-old me expected to be, and finally became. But it took a while.

I have chosen to build my professional life from non-traditional roles: the Navy, security and intelligence, the Coast Guard, and now defence. Along

Don't change yourself for anyone else. Pretty doesn't last. Popularity is transient. Being kind does not make you a pushover. Illness does not make you broken.

the way, my career cadence was two steps forward, one step back. Self-doubt accompanied me for many of those years. "Smart? No, not enough." "Pretty? No, not enough." "Good parent? No, working too much." The self-doubt was perversely compounded by conscious decisions to slow my career to steer our family through some difficult times marked by profound illness. During those years, self-doubt smothered all that had been wonderful in four-year-old me. Adult me had her own mantra: *Fit in. Fit in. Fit in.*

Even as I worked to be that elusive "enough," I faced chauvinism and misogyny in my career, doors that weren't open to me, and backlash against opinions I wasn't supposed to have. It was exhausting—and, in fact, still is. Adult me became angry—angry at myself. Angry because I was trying to be something I wasn't, trying to hang on to things in life that are fleeting and, ultimately, unimportant. I didn't want to live that way anymore. So I stopped, and reverted to the life lessons I had known by heart at age four. Be curious. Have opinions. Be yourself.

Looking back, I wonder why I tried so hard to fit into an unreasonable and undefined standard. I smile; that doesn't mean I lack gravitas. I love my family; that doesn't mean I'm not dedicated to my career. I have opinions; that doesn't make me strident. I am exactly the person I am meant to be, supported by an exceptional and intelligent husband and two impressive kids.

When I speak with young women, I'm often asked what advice I would give my nineteen-year-old self. The answer is, "None. She wouldn't have listened anyway." But I would tell my twelve-year-old self to stay the course. Don't change yourself for anyone else. Pretty doesn't last. Popularity is transient. Being kind does not make you a pushover. Illness does not make you broken.

Be curious. Be opinionated. Be who you were meant to be.

In 1984, JODY THOMAS joined the naval reserves straight out of university and was among the first women to serve on a Canadian military vessel. She began her federal public service career in 1988. Following a series of increasingly demanding security operations roles, Thomas became the first female commissioner of the Canadian Coast Guard in 2015. In 2017, she moved to national defence as senior associate deputy minister, and was subsequently appointed as deputy minister in September 2017.

TINA MOON

THIS IS GRADE school on picture day. Life in grade school is simple and fun, but in middle school and high school it becomes complicated and competitive—neither of which I am. This was a time when I did not internalize each moment and action of my life; it was before I moved to a big new city when I was eight, taking me from a small town in northern Ontario. Before I was the new kid in the class. Before I moved yet again to another new city at sixteen, leaving my boyfriend, best friend, and first job—and again the experience of being the new kid in class. This was before that embarrassing moment, reading aloud in English class just before my high school graduation. And it was before those around me, people who I trusted and loved, would doubt my decisions and choices, always having opinions yet not listening to mine.

As painful and humorous as those moments are to recall, I am grateful for them. Through these experiences I learned how to cope when I couldn't control the circumstances around me. These moments forced me to become comfortable with being uncomfortable.

The next photo you'll see was taken after I turned forty. It was after I started a new job in a new country, with three times the earning potential of my previous role. After becoming a wife and a mother. After travelling alone to Europe to start a new job. At some point as I was growing up and

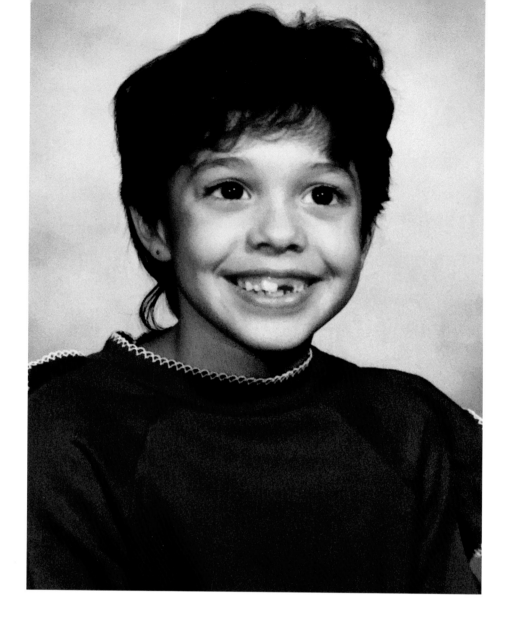

becoming this adult version of my myself, I began to believe in myself. I began to believe others when they told me I did a good job. I began to trust others who wanted to help me; I chose to be open and vulnerable to those around me. I started to think about my strengths, and began to focus on becoming better. I no longer tried to hold myself to perfection, or criticized my own approach. I learned from my mistakes, even if they were big, embarrassing, or stupid, because there is always something to learn from such moments, and from the people around me.

Through these experiences I learned how to cope when I couldn't control the circumstances around me. These moments forced me to become comfortable with being uncomfortable.

I realized that everything I have gone through in my life has provided me with the competencies of coping, resilience, optimism, and openness, which have all led to my personal successes, along with my failures. It has all led me to understand what is most important to me: my family, continuous learning, and progress—always moving forward.

All the while I am wondering: How long will this last? Am I good enough, deserving of this? And all the while grateful for everything I have and, especially, for the love of my family.

—————

TINA MOON, CHRL, ACC, works in human resources at Avast Software. She is Canadian, and now lives in the Bay Area of California with her husband and son. Outside of work, Moon cherishes time spent with her family, which includes travelling with her boys—anywhere near the ocean or experiencing new places they haven't been before.

KIM FURLONG

I **MAKE FRIENDS LAUGH** when I first tell them I am a bit shy. But anyone who spends time with me knows that, while I am outgoing and love people, my shyness is real. And while very few can sense it, I still, at times, have to talk to myself before a public or networking event, telling myself to shake it off and just do it; the first part to success is just showing up.

I grew up on the Gaspé coast of Quebec, raised by parents who were both entrepreneurs. I believe the woman I am today was created by the environment I grew up in. My parents told me that education was the key to my success, gave me room to make mistakes with no expectation of who I should be but myself, and worked extremely hard, teaching by example. Intelligence is often measured as book smart versus street smart. I believe I am both, and that I owe to my folks.

I worked in my parents' restaurant from the age of nine until I was in graduate school. I worked long hours. I worked hard. So much so that nothing since has ever been so physically testing, and any time I think I'm tired I go back to those summer days when my friends were on a beach and I was waiting tables, and remind myself how lucky I am. I am lucky because of

the work ethic that was gifted to me then. I am lucky because I have a deep appreciation for my success. I can still hear my dad, Raymond, say to me: "You have to go to school and you have to go *all* the way." And that I did.

I am also lucky because I was privy to failure early in my life. Running a business means taking risks, and every member of my family was a contributing player to that restaurant's success—and a witness to the trials and tribulations: bankruptcy, starting anew, and finding ways to make things work. Over the years, with every big decision, with every risk I had to take, it all came down to one simple question: What's the worst that can happen? Resourcefulness is the answer. There is always someone willing to help or teach you, and you simply have to ask.

A dynamic leader with political acumen, KIM FURLONG offers a unique combination of government, corporate, and trade association experience. As CEO of CVCA, she is the spokesperson for Canadian Private Capital and advocates for the best investment policy environment. Prior to this role, Furlong oversaw external affairs for Amgen Canada.

KAREN GREVE YOUNG

I **N GRADE 9,** I went out for the crew team at my public high school and it changed my life. Rowing was an awakening for me—a sport that rewarded effort and perseverance over natural coordination and ability. I set my sights for the US junior national team and trained with an intensity I'd never known. Two years later, I was on a junior national development team that beat senior women to win gold at the American Rowing Championships.

At age seventeen, I went into the junior national team selection camp with the third-best erg (rowing machine) score in the US for women aged eighteen and under. But my hopes were cut short when I suffered rib stress fractures in training. I would not be representing my country in France that summer.

I kept rowing—and was recruited by Harvard University to row for Radcliffe, the women's crew team. In my sophomore year, I made the top boat, our varsity 8+. But injury struck again—this time, overuse injuries in my knees, plus a recurrence of the rib stress fractures that had cut my junior national team dream short.

I lost my seat in the varsity boat, but with the support of my coaches and the reluctant permission of my worried parents, I competed at Eastern Sprints with our 2v boat. It was excruciating to even get into the boat, much less race, but I gutted it out through the heats and finals and our boat earned the silver medal. I had to ice my ribs and knees every time I rowed.

I often say that the goals I haven't achieved, despite massive effort, have shaped me at least as much as my successes. Those times are when I pushed my pain threshold, developed a keen appreciation for the power of teams, and learned that while I could rebound from some setbacks, sometimes I needed to reset my expectations and find new paths.

A pivotal reset came two years after my MBA, when it became clear that my mother's ovarian cancer was terminal. I wasn't her caregiver, just her daughter who loved her and wanted time with her—time that my full-time consulting role was denying me.

Looking back today, my decision to stop working for a few years to focus on family and write a shared memoir with my mother—which seemed like such a massive career derailment at the time—did more for my long-term success than a few consulting cases ever could have. It marked the beginning of my professional transition from business to non-profit management focused on causes that matter to me, which I love and have been doing ever since.

My mom passed away in 2004, a few days after learning the name of her first grandchild—my son Jeffrey, who was born four months later. I was with her in her final days and self-published our book in 2011.

Today, I am honoured to serve as CEO of Futurpreneur, a national non-profit that helps young Canadian entrepreneurs launch successful businesses. Although I no longer row, I still exercise most days, focused on staying injury-free as part of a full and fulfilling life.

It's easy to look back and say that this path, and all its twists and turns, made sense all along. But it wasn't obvious at the time. It required serendipity and hard work as dual career drivers, the support of family and friends along the way, and the conviction that things will work out in the end if we treat failures as learning opportunities in disguise.

KAREN GREVE YOUNG is the CEO of Futurpreneur Canada, a national organization dedicated to helping young entrepreneurs launch successful businesses. She previously held management and strategy roles in Toronto, San Francisco, New York, and London, most recently at MaRS Discovery District, and co-authored a cancer memoir with her late mother. Greve Young holds an MBA from Stanford and a BA from Harvard. She is the proud mother of Jeffrey and Kathryn.

JULIA ELVIDGE

IN HIGH SCHOOL, I didn't stand out. I didn't have the best marks, but I didn't have the worst. I was active, but I wasn't a jock. I didn't really know what I wanted to do with the rest of life, but my mom always said "you are going to university"—so I did. She wanted me to study sciences so I could get a job with a good salary and be independent—so I did.

Growing up in Waterloo, Ontario, I walked through the university campus to get to my high school. There were so many different degrees! I couldn't decide. Eventually, I settled on optometry. Later, attending pre-optometry science at the University of Waterloo, I survived first year only to be told that we now needed *two* years of pre-opt before I could apply to the program. Six years of university before a degree instead of five—no way! Much to my mother's disappointment, I dropped out in the middle of second year.

After working for a while, I managed to get in a scholarship program at the university in Trois-Rivières. It was an exchange program, and I taught English discussion classes while I lived in the community, and learned French. I met an electrical engineering student who spoke very little English but, incredibly, he was learning engineering from English textbooks. Bored one afternoon, I started reading one. When I asked him questions, he told me I was too stupid to learn engineering. I was shocked.

That shock became a challenge, and I started researching engineering degrees. I decided on biomedical engineering. At that time, I could only do it as a master's degree. I needed an undergraduate degree in electrical engineering first. So I went back to Waterloo, and after some hard work, I got myself accepted.

The engineering program at UW was only given as a co-op program. I'm not sure if I would have finished my degree if not for this program. I loved the work environments, I was inspired by the people I worked with, and I fell in love with semiconductor chip design. I never made it to my biomedical master's degree because I didn't need it anymore. I had found my career.

I was still an anomaly as a woman engineer, and most of my colleagues and customers were male. I was challenged as a woman in this environment, but it was an intellectual challenge.

My dad was an electrical engineer, but as a teenager, I wasn't sure what he did. I thought his job must be uninteresting and cold, with no social impact. I realize now that I needed to humanize engineering to consider it as a career option (which I did by specializing in biomedical). Later, I learned that my father was responsible for the complete overhaul of our country's air traffic navigation system in the 1980s. It taught me how engineering is always making an impact—in this case, passenger safety.

I did not know that I would find microchips fascinating—but I did. I had multiple job offers when I graduated. At that time, I was still an anomaly as a woman engineer, and most of my colleagues and customers were male. I was challenged as a woman in this environment, but it was an intellectual challenge. Usually, they just wanted to know if I knew my stuff, so I made sure that I knew it!

I went on to become an engineering manager and enjoyed working with my team (typically, all male). I jumped on new opportunities and tried new

things like marketing and sales, and being head of a business unit. Eventually, I became president, and I worked with the senior management team to define the strategy and culture of an organization. Quite a journey for the teenager who didn't stand out in high school.

———————

JULIA ELVIDGE is a strategic advisor, board member, and investor for high-technology companies. Educated as an electrical engineer, she started designing microchips before moving into the business side of technology. As president and co-founder, Elvidge helped build Chipworks into an industry leader delivering IP and technology services to global electronics companies.

PAMELA MCDONALD KUHNE

MAYBE IT WAS the Bionic Woman—Jaime Sommers and her amazing physical abilities—or maybe it was those spectacular 1976 Olympics, with Nadia Comăneci and her perfect 10s. I was far too young to be in the Games, but I was old enough to feel the energy and excitement in Montreal that summer. Whatever the origin, I knew that to be in the Olympics would be an incredible achievement. There was just one catch: as I got older, the enormity of the challenge terrified me. I was neither bionic nor athletically gifted. So, short of a miracle, I had no pathway to reach that dream.

The curious thing about opportunity is that it often comes bundled as a box of fear. To achieve big accomplishments requires stepping out of your comfort zone and becoming vulnerable to failure. And so, in the winter of 2012, while I was living in London, England—married, busy with my career and travels, my plate already bountiful—I learned of a call for dancers to volunteer their skills for the opening ceremonies of the London Paralympic Games. And I applied.

Here's the thing—from 1976 to 2012, I never trained as a dancer, nor did I perform in any big play or theatrical production. So without a doubt I was unqualified. Plus, I was scheduled to fly out with my husband on a very early overseas flight on the actual day of the auditions.

Yet, I still went for it. I was terrified, because I knew that this role was so outside of my skill set and abilities. We managed to move the travel to the following morning.

So I go, and I give it a go. I meet people from all over the world, both in line, and in the small groups they put us in for the auditions—which are not just an hour or two, but all day. Everyone I meet is a singer, a dancer, a juggler, or even a circus performer, one with a flexibility that seems otherworldly. I am so clearly out of my lane. During the actual judging, I'm awkward, stiff, and generally worse than dreadful. "Clumsy" is probably a generous description of my performance. I am not of the same calibre as my mates. No one other than my husband Eric would ever know about this humiliation.

And yet, four months later I got the official offer from the Games committee. That summer was spent in nondescript warehouses in the east of London, learning our routine. I was part of the very first group that opened the 2012 Paralympic Games—it was a dance routine set to Rihanna's "Umbrella."

Nothing could prepare me for the feeling of stepping out onto the stadium field and hearing sixty thousand people roar as they see us in our bright costumes. We stayed in place as Stephen Hawking addressed the crowd and then, with that six minutes, I made it to the Olympics, as a participant rather than a spectator. All because I stared down my fear—and said, "Why not?"

As an accredited sommelier and as a trainee glider pilot, PAMELA MCDONALD KUHNE believes that learning continues beyond the classroom, and inspiration can be found in multi-disciplinary exploration. She has published on incentive mechanisms for professionals in healthcare delivery and lectured graduate students in London and Gibraltar. She is the founder of civichealth.ca and a Fellow of the Royal Society for the Encouragement of Arts, Manufactures and Commerce, a 250-year-old organization dedicated to exploring new ideas that will provide pragmatic solutions to modern problems.

VALERIE FOX

THIS FIRST PICTURE is from when I was a little girl, and in the second I am in my forties and on skates. The second was taken by a news photographer in a Michigan town my husband and I were visiting. We were surprised to see it in the local paper the next day. Certainly, my husband was a much better skater, but I got the photo op. Go figure.

I was a middle child and the oldest girl of three children, growing up in the 1960s in New York. I remember being happy, boisterous, and constantly stepping out of the lines my mother drew for me. She hoped I would be a frilly, girly type, who enjoyed dressing up in patent leather shoes. But that wasn't me.

Like a typical middle child, I tended to vie for attention by competing with my older brother on the academic side, and competing with my younger sister by being "creatively" adventurous and precocious. There are likely better ways to get noticed, but this behaviour seemed to serve me as a child, carrying me first into adulthood, and now as a senior and grandmother.

The interesting result is that I tried all kinds of things, finding many I wasn't good at until, to my delight, I found what I was good at. This was a

useful method for someone who constantly felt like the odd man out. I was extremely tall throughout my childhood, and grew to be six-foot-one.

The teens can be a difficult time for many. For me, they created a major bump in the road—where being "normal" and like everyone else mattered—and they shattered my confidence. I spent a large part of that time alone and unhappy.

When I was sixteen, my mother did something amazing. She enrolled me in a summer program in an out-of-town university for art. She knew I needed to re-believe in myself—to draw outside the lines again. And she believed I would be able to do this by being in a new environment, one that was filled with people who could experiment with art and life.

It was a huge turning point. I made many friends, and explored many aspects of relationship building, art, and design. Much to my parents' chagrin, I came back braless and a vegetarian. But, to their delight, I also came back happy and confident.

Thinking about this, I see the budding entrepreneur—failing lots of times, but picking myself up and trying again. I guess I could have included a photo of myself at sixty-five; however, I don't skate now on real skates, just metaphorical ones—zigzagging through the bumps, and constantly moving forward.

VALERIE FOX is an entrepreneurial experience designer, community builder, supporter, and coach. She is co-founder of the DMZ at Ryerson University, which was named the top university business incubator in North America and third in the world by UBI under her tenure. Fox is now founder of The Pivotal Point, where she fosters collisions between technology, people, and process to form cultures of economic and social success worldwide.

SHINE

"UNTIL ALL OF US HAVE MADE IT, NONE OF US HAVE MADE IT."

———

Rosemary Brown

Sharing Our Flame

"**A** CANDLE LOSES NOTHING by lighting another candle"—this is a favourite saying of mine. I love the idea of giving of ourselves. Nothing is lost when one candle lights another. Its light is not diminished; rather, more light is created. Buddha said that thousands of candles can be lit from a single candle, and the life of that candle will not be shortened by these actions. The notion that happiness only increases by being shared resonates with me. Sometimes, the circumstances we face can make it hard to want to share the light. Have you heard of the "sisterhood ceiling"? According to research, it's a phenomenon that sees women preventing other women from advancing in the workplace. Apparently this is a thing, but I have not seen it in my life.

When opportunities are scarce, competition increases, and it can make some women less supportive of other women. It may exist, but the women profiled here are all about lighting others up. They're examples of the Shine Theory. The term was coined by Aminatou Sow and Ann Friedman. It's the idea of being intentional about supporting other women in their success. Whenever I'm addressing an audience of women, I remind them that we have the chance, through our own actions, to redefine the narrative that says women don't support each other. In my experience, and directly in my career, I've been the lucky beneficiary of unrelenting support from incredible

women in my circle. They've pushed me forward, propped me up, and cheered me on. I do the same for them. With intent. Women who use the Shine Theory want to have their close female friends and colleagues excel. It's the opposite of the sisterhood ceiling.

The Shine Theory offers a way to push out insecurity and competitiveness at work and in life, and instead create a coalition of women collaborators focused on helping each other. Here are stories of women who shine, and who shine the light for others, so thousands of candles can be lit and more light is created as they move fearlessly through the world.

JANICE

PASCALE FOURNIER

I WAS RAISED IN Abidjan, Ivory Coast, within a family that encouraged my exposure to different cultures and languages, so I gained an understanding of others from an early age. These influences profoundly affected my identity and leadership values. "Once social change begins, it cannot be reversed," wrote César Chávez. "You cannot uneducate the person who has learned to read. You cannot humiliate the person who feels pride. And you cannot oppress the people who are not afraid anymore."

My own academic and professional vision has blossomed out of this spirit of positive social change, one that promotes emancipation and greater opportunities for the women and men hidden behind Chávez's statement. My grandmother also played a significant role in my life, and enabled me to have a voice. Grand-maman Lamothe, the feminist, the friend, the confidante, the mentor. She was a compassionate leader whose journey was to bring meaningful impact to the world. She was most at home working with and for others, sharing their dreams and helping their success.

She ran for municipal politics in Quebec, using her deceased husband's first and last names. I framed a poster from that campaign, and it now hangs in my living room. It reads: "Votons Madame Paul Lamothe." As a young girl, I was sad to think that my loving and most extraordinary grandmother would use a male identity in order to be elected as a woman. It simply didn't feel right. Every time I asked about it, she reminded me that women only obtained the right to vote in 1940 in Quebec.

My grandmother was physically short, but seemed like a giant to me. I followed her from small meeting to big gathering. She would say, with a soft voice, "Listen, observe, and take it all in." This was our secret. On her dying bed, Grand-maman Lamothe took her Governor General's medal and placed it inside my tiny, twelve-year-old hands. "God is calling me now," she said. "I have to go. I will watch you from above. Make sure to always bring a positive difference. This will be my legacy to you." This last conversation was worth all the pain of letting her go. From that moment on, with her heavy medal becoming mine, I knew I had a mandate. I, too, would look for the brightest of stars. And make them shine.

On September 23, 2016, I took my two eldest sons, Charles and Pierre, on a trip to Scotland to participate in the signing of the St Andrews Declaration on a Shared Humanity. It was a classic Grand-maman Lamothe moment. I had come all the way from Canada to attend this event, as part of my work with religious women around the world. And yet I found myself bringing my boys, and whispering to them: "Listen, observe, and take it all in." I could see my grandmother in me, and felt as if she was watching from above.

I have taken Charles, Pierre, and my baby, Henry, on many trips to share my research on women's rights in Europe. I teach my boys the value of making a difference. We can gain a lot from consulting and welcoming children into the decision-making process, because it teaches them how to be great leaders.

I recognize the influence my grandmother had in my own life and the values she taught me. She has shaped the woman I am today, and the way I have chosen to raise my children.

———————

DR. PASCALE FOURNIER began as president and CEO of the Pierre Elliott Trudeau Foundation in July 2018, taking bold steps to modernize and innovate the foundation's programs. Previously, Fournier was a full professor and Research Chair in Legal Pluralism and Comparative Law at the University of Ottawa. She holds a PhD in Law from Harvard University.

MEENA ROBERTS

IN THIS FIRST photo, I am seventeen, maybe eighteen. I am representing Seethalakshmi Ramaswami College in an Inter-Collegiate Debating competition being held at an all-men's engineering college in Tiruchi. I won some award for debating that day, but I don't remember what exactly. What I do remember is a huge audience of boys, five or six male judges in the front row, and the cacophony of applause, chuckles, catcalls, and whistles as I made my way to the podium. It is my most familiar memory of my growing years: always a knot in my stomach, but pushing on nevertheless.

Seeing that picture, my stomach still tightens. That girl is not just standing in front of an audience. She is standing up to a culture that is hostile to girls, that directs who she can and cannot be, daily. She must remain steely, make her point, standing alone if needed, and ready to take the flak that comes with it—gossip, threats, beatings, shaming words, and ostracism.

You have to understand the India she was born into, in 1961. The literacy rate for women was below 10 percent; less than 4 percent of girls enrolled in university; female participation in paid work was 5 percent; child marriage was normal; arranged marriage was a requirement, and bride burning for dowry or disobedience was common. Girls lived and died as extensions of their father, then husband; an accessory to a man's life. My sisters and I were born into this India. Luckily, to parents who wanted better for their girls.

You are a girl, so you are not that special. The rates of female infanticide prove it so. As a girl you are born with a plan and a script in place. It is the

If you can't break the glass ceiling, find a way to climb on top of it.

same script that millions of girls share, no exceptions or deviations allowed. Keep your head low, eyes downcast, mouth quiet, in your box, and never dream of blowing it open.

I didn't know then that this girl would blow the box wide open. She would win an international scholarship. ("Scholarships are wasted on a girl," he said. "How would you know, Sir," she replied, "if you've never given it to a girl?") She would board a flight (her first one); go alone, unchaperoned as a single unmarried female (unheard of); support herself through a degree (sometimes just one cheque away from homelessness); work her way to Harvard (what? Who would want to marry her now?); refuse arranged marriage (causing her parents so much pain); have a "love" marriage, and be shunned from family and community for a decade.

I also didn't know then that the girl who wanted to be "citizen of the world" would marry a Canadian (non-Hindu, non-vegetarian, non-Brahmin, not rich), have a mixed race son, adopt a daughter from China, and have Christian, Hindu, and Jewish godchildren. A multicultural vision that defied the script she was born with.

Her life was so far off script, her communities in Canada and India kept asking: What faith will your children learn? What religion will you practice? What about your culture? What about your people? But, by seventeen, she had figured out that her religion is compassion, her faith was her conscience, her people included everyone, and her culture was openness. With time, her family agreed and embraced.

Now, as an adult, there is a different kind of knot I must untangle, as a woman and a visible minority. I quit a career I loved in a "Big 6" firm because the bias was simply too big to take on alone. "We are thinking of adding female partners in our ranks but not ones like you," said the partner from Bay Street, in his bow tie, in 1992. Self-employment was my answer—from glass ceiling to open sky. It is a risk I could afford to take, but I know other minority women can't always. The statistics are clear. Despite education and language proficiency, minority women face employment gaps, wage gaps, promotion gaps, and are underrepresented in management and C-suites. Personally, what I couldn't do through C-suites, I decided to do through sitting on boards. If you can't break the glass ceiling, find a way to climb on top of it.

In the photo above, I am still standing at the podium, forty years later. But, in place of the finger wagging, there is a smile. I am speaking as chair of the board of Ashbury College, at its 124th graduation ceremonies. There are no catcalls, this time. I am highlighting our achievements, in inclusion—transitioning from an all-boys school to include girls, increasing financial assistance to include lower income students, expanding global reach to include students from more than fifty countries. I know my voice and work played a part.

Today, the country is different, the time is different, but the biases and boxes are similar. I have the same job of trying to open minds and open doors, but this time, it's not for myself. I have championed the hiring of

She is standing up to a culture that is hostile to girls, that directs who she can and cannot be, daily. She must remain steely, make her point, standing alone if needed, and ready to take the flak that comes with it . . .

women and minorities on male-only fire and police services, championed access to training and job opportunities for new immigrants; after-school programs for all kids; training programs and scholarships in community housing buildings; funding schools and homes for destitute children in South Asia, and vocational training for women and girls there.

As I start my third chapter in life, my work continues. The raging fire in me is now a calm flame. I have grown from lone warrior to community builder. There is no fame or fortune in what I do, but there is great satisfaction in being a voice for access and inclusion. I fly when others lift off.

————

MEENA ROBERTS has a thirty-year career working as a management consultant providing governance, strategy, and policy advice to the Canadian government and the non-profit sector in Ottawa and India. She has also served as a community leader on numerous boards and councils that champion better access to education, healthcare, housing, and skills training for the vulnerable. Roberts holds graduate degrees from Harvard University and the University of British Columbia.

CHAMIKA AILAPPERUMA

I WAS THE FIRST daughter to immigrant parents from Sri Lanka who were newcomers to Canada in the 1970s, and a sense of adventure and discovery underpinned much of my early childhood. When they first arrived, my father worked for the Sri Lankan embassy and we belonged to a small, tight-knit Sri Lankan community in Ottawa. I remember many outings to Ottawa parks and short road trips with other Sri Lankan families as my parents and their friends took in the vastness of their new home country and its breathtaking, unfamiliar scenery. In most of the photos of me as a very young girl, I am singing or talking—I've always had a voice that I used to be heard!

When I was four, soon after my sister was born, my father lost his job and our family story took a turn for uncertainty. At the age of forty, he went back to school to become an accountant. He couldn't find a job in Ottawa, so when I was eight we moved to Edmonton and, after a year of working in a small business there, my father opened his own accounting firm. The entrepreneurial route agreed with him, despite the ups and downs it created in our family life. As a testament to his pioneering spirit, his business is still standing thirty-five years later.

But neither Ottawa nor Edmonton were welcoming to people of colour like my family—many of my memories are filled with openly racist events, and I didn't understand why people called us names or disliked us because of the colour of our skin. During such ignorant episodes, I sensed and saw a twisted ugliness coming from these negative, aggressive, and violent people. I also knew, on some level, that the ugliness wasn't directed at us as people; rather, it came from fear of the change my family and I brought with us, and the unknown we represented.

Through those experiences, I became an advocate for acknowledging how we are all human and that we all win when we choose to see the positive possibilities in the face of change. Being relentless about expressing gratitude and appreciation for diversity and including others continues to inform my actions in the face of adversity and injustice, just as my voice continues to develop and amplify.

Today, my commitment to being a guide for those navigating change is possible because I see such a bright future, thanks to the many talented leaders among us, and our ability to unite and create. I feel the same sense of adventure and exploration I felt as a child as I use my voice to speak up about the work we must continue to do in Canada to advance women's leadership and ensure equity and inclusion for women of colour. On this journey, I've had the honour and privilege to cross paths with incredible role models, mentors, and true champions who have shaped my voice and multiplied my opportunities for success. From the examples I've benefitted from, I pay it forward to the many different people I mentor and guide their voices to speak and be heard.

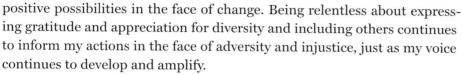

CHAMIKA AILAPPERUMA is an innovation leader with expertise in business transformation, change management, and strategic partnership building across several sectors. Ailapperuma has also been a passionate and committed mentor to many people and organizations throughout her career.

ASTRID PREGEL

"HOW IS THIS possible?" I am wondering in this photo. The year is 1996. I have recently learned that women hold ownership in one-third of Canada's small businesses, and the research is showing me something eerie. It seems like no one in the federal government knows this startling fact, let alone understands what the implications could be for the country's economy and for our international trade strategy.

"Could I really be all alone on this file?" I thought. True, I was the first woman appointed to the level of minister counsellor in Canada's Washington embassy, and the first woman to run the embassy's commercial programs. But surely something so important would have a prominent place in developing Canada's commercial and economic policies, wouldn't it? And so began my journey into what I would coin "Feminomics"—the intersection of gender perspectives with economics.

As it turned out, I *was* pretty much alone. But, fortunately, with the support of Ambassador Raymond Chrétien, the unflagging confidence of the Royal Bank of Canada's legendary Charlie Coffey, an ace team of embassy officials, and several out-of-the-box-thinking politicians—including the minister of international trade, Sergio Marchi—in 1997 we were able to launch Canada's first business women's trade mission, 125 women strong. A change of this magnitude for women entrepreneurs was not to take place again in Canada for twenty years! It would take decades to learn—

often painfully—that for a woman's voice to be heard, let alone for it to influence global change, powerful male supporters are necessary.

The impact of our work in Washington continues to ripple through to the present day. Our trade mission entrepreneurs received press that took their impact far beyond their initial goal of expanding their businesses. Several federal bureaucrats had their own aha moments, and I was able to marvel as support unfolded for further research and the creation of the Business Women in International Trade program at Global Affairs Canada. New funding for programs became available for women entrepreneurs, and within a few years Status of Women Canada would lead the funding for the creation of WEconnect International in Canada, the link for business women to the US and global supply diversity markets.

Today, Feminomics is evolving again, examining entirely new ways to organize outside of, or parallel to, the capitalist system. How this might look is not yet clear, but what I do know is that "add women and stir" is not enough. I also know that we don't need to "fix" women to fit into an economic system created for men, by men. What we need to do is look at systems that accommodate the natural strengths and talents of the entire population, not only the male half.

What I also did not realize in 1996 was that there is a price to pay for leading change that pushes at some of the very basic organizing principles of society—such as how we define what women and men are and what they do, and how women and men engage in economic activity and create prosperity. In my case, part of the price was surviving a nasty bureaucratic witch hunt. But I did survive, and I continue to thrive. The advantage of twenty-first century witch hunts is that the witch lives on to bring forward new challenges in new ways. The Feminomics Witch—that's me!

ASTRID PREGEL is a passionate advocate for the economic empowerment of women. She has spent most of the past twenty-five years studying, advocating, writing policy, and advising international organizations and governments on women's economic issues. Pregel is a career foreign service officer and president of Feminomics Ltd., a boutique consulting firm specializing in women's economic empowerment, leadership, and entrepreneurship.

CAROL DEVENNY

I WOULD DESCRIBE MYSELF as a forward thinker. By the age of twelve I knew I wanted to study at Queen's University (following a long line of family alumni), and by the age of fourteen I had decided to pursue a business degree. And so I did—in September 1978, I travelled from Edmonton, where I attended high school, to Kingston, where I joined the class of Queen's Commerce '82.

My fellow classmates of just under two hundred were terrific (and I don't just say that because I'm married to one), and many of us remain good friends. Our class was equally divided between male and female, something I didn't appreciate until I started working for a professional accounting firm, and both in the "bull pen" and with clients I found myself wondering where all the women had gone. I joined Price Waterhouse (now PwC) in June 1982, and my forward-thinking self boldly announced my intention to become a partner—only to be told the firm didn't have any in Canada. (The very first Canadian was made partner in 1985, the same year I became a chartered accountant.)

I wanted to differentiate myself (and, again, I was thinking ahead), so I obtained my Chartered Business Valuator certification, as well as my CPA in the US, and in 1995 I was admitted as a PwC partner.

Throughout my career, I was often the only female in a meeting—one of the most memorable moments was joining my fellow partners, all male, at a remote fishing camp. The satellite phone bill as I regularly checked in at home must have been outrageous!

Back then, I often found myself presenting to all-male audit committees and boards. One "seasoned" male board member asked me how I managed, given that men were generally better with numbers. I told him that, as it happens, I have always been good with numbers, but more importantly—as is the case with many women—I am very good with people, and that has been the key to my success.

I have always advocated for women in business, and particularly women in accounting and auditing. Anyone working with me knows that if they don't consider women for leadership roles, I will challenge them to. I have been a coach and mentor for many professional women over the years, and I'm so proud of what many have accomplished.

I have had an amazing, challenging, and rewarding professional career with PwC. I will soon be retiring, after thirty-eight years, and I'm looking forward to the next phase. I hope it will include the opportunity to serve on corporate boards, where I can continue to use my business skills, and help promote other women in the boardroom.

CAROL DEVENNY, FCPA, FCA, CBV, CPA (Illinois), ICD.D, is a partner with PwC. She has almost forty years of experience as a professional accountant, as well as with non-profit boards and audit committees—currently, she serves with the Ottawa Community Foundation and the International Women's Forum. In 2014, Devenny was named one of Canada's 100 Most Powerful Women by WXN.

TANYA VAN BIESEN

I COME FROM A family of three—two brothers and me—and we were all raised the same way. Our very Dutch parents expected us to work hard at school, attend university, and go out and build careers—all three of us. In this early picture you can see the ambition in my young face; I was taught that hard work was the critical ingredient to achieving success.

At university, I graduated at the top of my class. I then entered the work world and was soon on my way, keeping pace with my peers. I believed deeply that the harder and smarter I worked, the more successful I would be.

But here's the funny thing—when you believe in something so strongly, it's like you have blinders on; you don't necessarily see some of the things going on around you.

Shortly after starting my first job, I met my now husband at the same company. It was while we were on our first date that I learned he had been hired at a higher starting salary than I—for the identical position. At the time, I quietly laughed it off and told myself: "I'm sure there's a reason why; just put your head down and work harder." (Oh, and yes, I also made him pay for dinner.)

Eighteen years of hard work later, I was up for partnership in a global consulting firm alongside a male colleague. He and I had joined the firm at the same time and had been peer contributors in all respects. Yet in the middle of the process, one of the firm's senior partners shared that my path to partnership was being challenged. There was some concern that I, a mother

of two kids, wouldn't be able to keep up the pace of travel expected of a partner of a global firm.

I was stunned and confused. I knew that I was one of the busiest consultants in the office and had never hesitated to get on a plane for a client. More frustrating, I also knew that my colleague's path wasn't being challenged. Odd, because he was a father of three.

After documenting five years of business travel, and passionately making my case, I did in the end make partner. But I was now awake to the disparities in gender equity that had become impossible to ignore.

The blinders were off.

This second picture shows me today, finally at a place where my ambition and hard work have aligned in the most positive of ways, behind the ultimate goal: gender parity at all levels.

If I told you that, today, the majority of university graduates in Canada are women, you'd probably say, "Great, problem solved. All we have to do now is wait twenty-five years and those graduates will advance through our organizations and into leadership." Right?

Except women led university graduation even twenty-five years ago. And yet today, the overwhelming majority of corporate CEOs are men, and women still earn less. In short, progress for women continues to be slow.

This is why I have since left consulting to lead Catalyst in Canada. We are working hard to accelerate progress for women in the corporate world, and I have hope that we are heading in a good direction. This second picture shows me today, finally at a place where my ambition and hard work have aligned in the most positive of ways, behind the ultimate goal: gender parity at all levels.

TANYA VAN BIESEN is the executive director of Catalyst in Canada, working closely with leaders across the country to accelerate progress for women. She is a recognized and accomplished executive with twenty years of experience in the executive search sector, focusing on assignments at the board, CEO, and general management levels.

VENT

URE

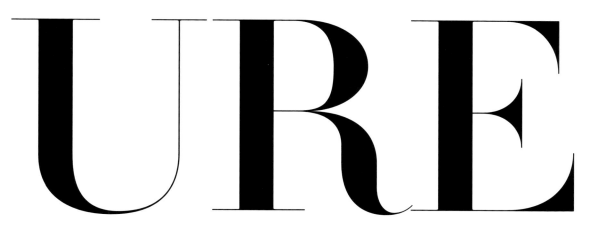

"NEXT TO TRYING
AND WINNING, THE
BEST THING IS
TRYING AND FAILING."

L.M. Montgomery

Sometimes "Fearless" Means "Fearing Less"

THE EMAIL INVITE I received was to come and speak in PNG. My first thought was *Yes!* My next thought was: Where exactly is PNG? Papua New Guinea is an island country in the southwestern Pacific Ocean, and a destination I had never contemplated. A quick Google search revealed fascinating facts about this faraway place, along with stories of cannibalism that were spread and made lurid across the colonial world. A country with 851 different languages, it remains one of the globe's least explored places, both culturally and geographically. Interestingly, up until 1933, seashells were used as the currency of the country. As someone who likes adventure, a place so far from my home, and so little travelled, had appeal. And yet, PNG is also often ranked as the worst place in the world for violence against women, with the capital, Port Moresby, holding an entrenched reputation as a dangerous place.

So, why would I agree to go there?

Susan Jeffers's bestselling book *Feel the Fear and Do It Anyway* reminds us that we can't wait for fear to go away before we act. Instead, we have to keep pushing ourselves forward to do more things we're afraid of, to prove to ourselves that we can handle all kinds of experiences—uncertainty, danger, loss, and more. With each new challenge, we build our confidence, and become more able to take on new and different obstacles. Fear doesn't go away, but, with practice, we get more comfortable with the feelings fear evokes in us.

I did feel the fear as I scrolled through the travel warnings, and then set my plans to go to PNG anyway. As a woman travelling alone, I took the necessary precautions. Nothing bad happened. Instead, I had tremendous experiences. I presented my research on women entrepreneurs, met incredible people from many different countries, and enjoyed a limited taste of a fascinating city.

Growth and comfort are in constant conflict. Creating the life I want to live has meant embracing courage. Again and again and again. Like all the women in this book, I've taken action despite my fears. Difficult circumstances and new challenges offer each of us the opportunity to experience tremendous personal growth. We don't need to think about our options as either-or choices, or worry about making the absolute best decision. Instead, like Jeffers suggests, when thinking about a decision, we can see an array of possibilities, and know that each offers the opportunity for growth and fulfillment. No choice is really a bad one, they are all merely pathways to different experiences.

When I finally landed at Jacksons International Airport in Port Moresby, I took a big breath, exhaled, and let my adventures begin ... just like, I'm sure, each of the venturing women who are profiled in this chapter.

JANICE

GIULIANA
MAZZETTA

AS A YOUNG girl, I was this photo—a rowdy tomboy wearing my tutu. I would play with my brother and the neighbourhood boys, then run inside to paint with my eyes closed or dress up my dolls. There were no boundaries to my identity—I could be who I wanted to be.

In many ways, I have my parents to thank. My mom, an eccentric artist, always encouraged creativity without self-consciousness. She would say, "Go wild, who cares how it turns out!" My dad, on the other hand, never made me feel different because I was girl; he was always encouraging me to swim another lap, feel proud to conquer those things that scare me (math!) and to dream big, then *bigger!*

Years passed and I found myself in Montreal, studying at McGill. By that time, I got swept into the uni life, and was suddenly insecure with my abilities as I compared myself to my peers. It was a formative first year, with a freshly separated family back home and all of my life looming in front of me. I think I had lost touch with that fire inside—that fire that approached life with fearlessness and playfulness.

My brother called me up one day and asked if we should do the Camino de Santiago. The previous summer, out of the blue, my father had completed this seemingly endless trek from France across Spain. My immediate impulse was "What! Me? Trek?" But the fire inside whispered encouragingly—GO!

Passing over the steep Pyrenees on our first day, I was filled with doubt and wanted to throw in the towel. But I persisted. Each day, I woke up renewed, and kept on. I followed a yellow arrow for hundreds upon hundreds of kilometres, only to find refuge in monasteries and hostels at night, Gregorian chants waking me at daybreak.

I made incredible friends along the way—from an astronomer to a priest to a veterinarian and a hairdresser. As one pilgrim said, we were "students participating in the university of life," each new friend like a professor. Discomfort and vulnerability became one with strength and resilience. Hundreds of stories shared full of wisdom from strangers, thousands of steps taken— and then, one day, I arrived at Santiago de Compostela with my own two feet.

I had reawakened that flame inside; I alone could be capable of so much more than I ever imagined. There were no boundaries to my identity.

Whether it's the girl in the tutu playing in the boys' club or the proud young woman on a thousand-kilometre trek, there is no greater freedom than realizing that we can relish in all that we are, boldly, and dare to explore the very depths our possibility.

The magic of the Camino has since called me back three times. And what I have realized is that we are always on a Camino. Looking up at the Milky Way from the Pyrenees, or seeing a yellow arrow spraypainted on a street in London, I know that the flame that lies in each of us is our guide in this journey of life. When we get off track, our flame calls us to renew our strength by stepping into the unknown—bravely. And, in doing so, we rediscover over and over again that there are no borders to be found.

And so when she calls, listen.

GIULIANA MAZZETTA is a creative strategist based in London with a background in business design and international development. Harnessing an eclectic mix of inspiration (ranging from the arts to technological innovation), Mazzetta loves to imagine how our world can thrive in the future, and then design products, services, strategies, and even stories to get us there.

JENNIFER COOKE

I HAVE ALWAYS BEEN drawn in by doorways. In every corner of the world I visit, I see doors of all shapes and sizes as a beautiful representation of the mantras for life that my parents taught me. My mother always told me, "You can do anything you want in life"—and this was a lesson that she taught by modelling it herself. Immigrating to Canada as a young girl, escaping difficult circumstances in a place where girls didn't have the same rights, she fought many challenges, overcame many barriers, and opened many closed doors. She was a great role model and a mentor to look up to—and to live up to.

I was also fortunate as a child that my parents enjoyed travelling, and every year they took my brother and me on an adventure to some new place. Early in life I learned to be open to new ideas and experiences, and I acquired the bug to try new things—because possibilities in life are endless and achievable! I have carried these lessons with me, and applied them every day.

Everywhere you go, a door leads you to a new place, a hidden space, or a new opportunity. Today, one door may be closed, but another will open to something even better. Throughout my life, I have found this to be a literal and a metaphorical truth. Several times along the journey of my life and career I have walked through new doors, tried something new in order

to reach new goals. Often, this meant leaving security—leaving my family and relocating to a new country on my own, leaving a well-paying job to try an entrepreneurial venture, leaving one industry to chase a passion, starting at the bottom again to learn and experience something new. Often, I chose seemingly opposite corners, not following the straight path, but instead trying a variety of different doors and trusting they would lead me to the right place—and, eventually, I found that they did.

For me, being fearless means taking a step through the next new door to see where it leads you, to challenge yourself to meet your next accomplishment in life. And when one path ends, to seek and find the door that will take you on a new path—not necessarily knowing where it will lead. It's only later you find that all the doors were connected, and they led you to the place you were meant to be.

Even today, I continue to look for doors, on my travels to new places and within my life and my work. I look to find the beauty, and the opportunity, in each of them.

JENNIFER COOKE is corporate lead of the Women in Trade strategy at Export Development Canada.

DENISE SHORTT

A S I GAZE at these two images of myself—the one here depicting my shy, introverted six-year-old self and the one on the following page taken many years later at the launch party for my first book—I wonder how I made it to that pivotal point in my career, and I remind myself of the courage it took that day to get behind the microphone and address a crowd of over two hundred people.

What you don't see in the second photo is my then fifty-six-year-old mother watching me proudly from the first row. Two years after it was taken, my mother succumbed to the killer cancer she already knew she had.

Now that I'm fifty-two and nearing the age my mother was when I lost her, I can look through the lens of that loss and reflect on it. But I can also celebrate the many ways she inspired me toward ambition, authenticity, and storytelling. As the second daughter of four children to two teenage small-town parents, I was lucky to have a mother who supported me in my dreams to leave that life behind, and become strong and fiercely independent.

When I was a teenager, my mother supported my desire to attend university, even though university and college grads were few and far between in our family tree. I worked hard for the privilege of earning my English degree, even though it meant working in a factory every summer from grade 9 onward. With that degree under my belt, I landed my first "real" job, at an educational publishing company, then worked my way upward, first as an associate and then senior editor. Finally, I was the youngest employee (at age

twenty-six) to be offered a publisher position. I didn't end up taking the role (it was too salesy) but decided instead to leave publishing for the tech world.

I had been bitten by the technology bug after managing the launch of the first-ever educational CD-ROM in Canada. The "information superhighway" was a new concept at that time and I wanted to navigate this new evolution. With little or no confidence that I would be accepted, I decided to apply to a brand-new technology master's program at Harvard University.

I went on to earn my degree at Harvard, then co-authored my first book, called *Technology with Curves: Women Reshaping the Digital Landscape.*

I was lucky to have a mother who supported me in my dreams to leave that life behind, and become strong and fiercely independent.

I knew at the time that very few women were working as designers and developers, and this had to change. The storyteller in me wanted to showcase these pioneering women in tech and celebrate their courageous accomplishments in a very male-dominated field. Specifically, I wanted to inspire younger women to embrace tech careers (as I did as an arts major) even if they weren't from traditional fields such as computer science or engineering.

Later, I co-authored a second book, called *Innovation Nation: Canadian Leadership from Java to Jurassic Park*. The Canadian government purchased ten thousand copies and sent them around the world to showcase Canadian innovation.

Now, I am vice president of diversity and inclusion at the leading national technology association, and I'm still committed to driving change for women in tech, and to supporting and showcasing female leaders, entrepreneurs, and innovators. My mother still watches over me, and I know she is spurring me on to continue to find new ways to face fears and find a way to give voice to the stories of others—even without a microphone.

DENISE SHORTT is vice president at ITAC and the co-author of *Technology with Curves* and *Innovation Nation*. She has a graduate degree from Harvard University and in 2011 she received a WCT Leadership award for her lifetime achievement of advancing women.

SABRINA FITZGERALD

AS A TEN-YEAR-OLD, I was adventurous around the neighbourhood, took trips with my family, and wanted to leave the nest on bigger adventures. When I had a chance to participate in Can-Amera Games, for competitive swimming, I was all in—despite the nerves, and despite apprehension about leaving the country without my parents.

At forty, I was offered an incredible opportunity to become the managing partner of our PwC offices in Ottawa. But this decision was no longer just about me and my desire for adventure: having a family of my own—my husband, Lee, and our two kids, Rae, 15, and Quinn, 10—we decided this was an adventure meant for all of us.

We were leaving my mom and dad, who lived down the road from us, and my brother and his family, who also lived minutes away, but there was doubt that this was the right move. We were so comfortable in Waterloo, Ontario. Who were we to think another city could be as great as what we knew? Our social circle, our network, our memories were all from Waterloo. Professionally, my connections were deep and rooted—I knew the business community, and they knew me.

Not unlike on that day I left for the Can-Amera Games, I wondered why I wanted to do something that was so scary, to leave the comforts of my

family, and my community. Back then, for the games, I was going to spend the week with a family I didn't know, but I knew it was going to be a growing opportunity. Little did I know at that time what a life lesson it would be.

In the photo on the facing page, I am returning from the games with grit and determination, medals hanging around my neck. I was proud to be home, having represented my swim team in the US. But I was also proud of having left the nest, and of making new connections.

Thirty years later, after many more small journeys, and now with my family by my side and support from my friends and community, I took the biggest leap into the unknown I'd encountered to date. Jumping into a new community—never having worked there, visited, or even knowing a soul—we packed up our family of four and embarked into a new chapter.

Professionally, this move was big. I had built my entire professional brand in a town that was now no longer relevant in the same way. My first year was a whirlwind and one of the hardest things I've had to go through. Working long days, weekends, and evenings to make the connections; working through strategy and reminding myself how it all tied to my values. It all came back to adventure. Life is an adventure, this is an adventure, Can-Amera was an adventure. So let's embrace that unknown!

What's next? I'm not sure, but I do know that jumping into this unknown territory was not so bad after all. It's taught us resilience and determination. We found a new community, a new social circle, and, together as a family, we've grown and learned from our experience.

———————

SABRINA FITZGERALD is the National Technology Sector leader at PwC Canada, as well as the managing partner of the National Capital Region. As an advocate for diversity in leadership, Fitzgerald is an active speaker, author, and mentor.

JODI KOVITZ

I HAVE TWO PICTURES that were taken more than twenty years apart, but they perfectly highlight how we always have the opportunity to choose the positive mindset.

The first picture is from a canoe trip I took when I was sixteen. The thirteen-day trip included a portage, which required me to carry a fifty-pound canoe for almost four miles. At the time I was in a panic about how I would conquer this feat, and I was convinced I needed someone to help me. I was filled with doubt, and skepticism at my ability to do this on my own.

When the moment came to start the portage, I realized that no one was coming to my rescue, and that finishing this task was solely dependent on me pushing myself to my limits and truly believing in my abilities, one step at a time. Those four miles were long and hard, but when I reached the end I was filled with immense joy and pride. This was also the moment I realized how dangerous self-doubt can be; it almost crippled me. I go back to this moment as a beacon that reminds me I can do anything I think I can.

This next photo, taken in 2017, happens to be one of my favourite pictures of myself. Yet, when I think about that moment, I know I was in a place of transition. Emotionally, I was right back to where sixteen-year-old canoe-trip me was. I had just started #movethedial and decided to leave a stable career to embark on a journey that I truly believed in. While I was determined to succeed, doubt had crept in again, secretly.

These are also stories I share with my daughter, because it's important for her to know that while every person has moments of fear, those moments don't define you or your path.

But this time, I had learned that the limits I set on what I can do are simply my own perception. Starting #movethedial was a risk, and it pushed my limits in ways that sometimes made me feel extremely uncomfortable—but I knew I had endured many years of failures, scars, and wounds and yet had always found myself in a much better place than where I began. The woman on that couch did not stay in a state of self-doubt for long; instead, she leaned into her fear, dreamed up a plan for #movethedial, and set out to get it, one step at a time.

Looking back on both of these experiences, I can see how pivotal they were. They taught me important lessons about navigating fear and personal limits, and I often think back to these moments when I find myself stuck. These are also stories I share with my daughter, because it's important for her to know that while every person has moments of fear, those moments don't define you or your path, and they certainly can't stop you from being a phenomenal woman.

JODI KOVITZ is the founder and CEO of #movethedial, a global movement dedicated to advancing the participation and leadership of all women in tech. In 2017, Kovitz was recognized by the Women's Executive Network as one of Canada's Top 100 Most Powerful Women, and in 2018 as one of the Top 25 Women of Influence by Women of Influence Canada.

BARBARA FAULKENBERRY

WHAT AN UNEXPECTED journey! It began as a leap of faith into the complete unknown. It was time to pick a college—but where to go? Lots of brochures arrived in the mail, but nothing grabbed my imagination.

Then, a picture on the front page—women marching for the first time up the "Bring Me Men" ramp as they entered the US Air Force Academy! Fascinating, unique, a bit scary, and a complete unknown to me. I had no understanding of the military, but I flew off to Colorado Springs.

My childhood in Clearwater, Florida, was somewhat routine, but there were glimpses into the person who would someday take this "road less traveled": writing a "book" when I was six years old; organizing a fundraiser for muscular dystrophy at thirteen; owning my own lawn mowing business in high school; Florida State racquetball women's champion at seventeen; graduating salutatorian of my class.

What type of life did I want for myself? I really had no idea back then, but I definitely didn't want boring, routine, typical.

Stepping out to attend a military academy, with all of its demands, restrictions, and incredible opportunities, was definitely not typical. Where else would a college education include soaring, parachuting, survival and unarmed combat training, travelling around the world, and pugil stick competitions (like swordfighting but with large sticks shaped like Q-tips).

A series of experiences and opportunities along the journey of my military career provided me with skills: to fight off a rapist; to respond to the Dhahran bombing and move my KC-135 tanker unit to a remote Saudi airfield virtually overnight; to represent the US government in arms-control talks in Vienna; to provide opening remarks at the International Military Conference on HIV/AIDS in Maputo, Mozambique; to respond to a break of diplomatic relations with Kyrgyzstan and relocate all air logistics operations to another Middle Eastern country across the Persian Gulf without missing a single combat sortie.

The young woman who stepped into the unknown, who became the winner of the "Big Bad Basic" pugil stick competition became a confident two-star general, ready to handle whatever new challenge came her way, whatever unique adventure she could create. I launched air refuelling sorties over New York in response to the attack on the United States on September 11, 2001; ran the Air Force's leadership development courses; took on the responsibility for all airlift, air refuelling, and aeromedical evacuations throughout Iraq and Afghanistan; led air, ground, and sea logistics for US military operations in Africa; and ultimately led a 37,000-person organization flying 1,100 aircraft to provide global air logistics for special operations, combat, and humanitarian operations.

I'm so glad I took that leap of faith!

MAJOR GENERAL BARBARA FAULKENBERRY is a senior executive with diverse accomplishments across sectors ranging from aerospace/defence to logistics to leadership development. Throughout her thirty-two-year military career, Faulkenberry's diverse responsibilities spanned the globe. She currently serves as an independent director for two public companies and five non-profit organizations. An athlete who enjoys biking and golf, Faulkenberry has hiked over a thousand miles on four different Camino de Santiago trails.

VERONICA VERED

ATTICUS, A CONTEMPORARY West Coast poet, once wrote about a woman who was powerful not because she *wasn't* afraid, but "because she went on so strongly / despite the fear." Living in this way has always been the only option for me.

I come from a long line of fearless women, but there is one in particular whom I must highlight: my mother. She first introduced me to the writing of Atticus, and she is the single most important and influential person in my life. My mother is the definition of fearless, and she has taught me everything I know today.

While I have always been determined to live fearlessly, this quality has often been tested—especially when I was a young girl. I was strong, passionate, and loved to lead, but this was sometimes mischaracterized as being bossy and pushy. The criticism may have weakened me at times, but it did not break me. I learned from it. It wasn't easy, but my mom persistently fostered these characteristics in me, and pushed me to be my absolute best. And she continues to do so today.

Many people choose to express themselves through fashion. When we were young, my fearless best friend and I loved to dress up for anything and everything. We loved finding new things to be interested in, whether it was cooking, sports, or, for a short while, sewing. For a time, we had access to fabric and a sewing machine—a dangerous combination. One day, Katrine decided to make me a "dress" of bright blue iridescent fabric, and I wore it with great

pride and confidence. I'm sure all the other girls judged it, but that didn't matter: my fearless best friend had made the most outrageously awesome dress, and she had made it just for me.

My latest test came recently, in 2018, when my soon-to-be husband and I decided to move to Dublin. He had just been accepted into medical school, and I into law school. Neither of us had ever been to Ireland, and we didn't know a single person there. But, together, we were able to move "across the pond," far away from both of our families, to start our own journey together.

My bold childhood fashion sense, standing up to criticism about my strong personality, my willingness to take on adventures in a new country: these were all frightening, but I faced every one. I still live fearlessly today, not by any innate choice, but absolutely thanks to the lessons of my mother. Like Atticus says, being fearless is not the absence of fear, but acting despite the fear. I like to think that I help inspire other people in my life to act despite the fear, and to be comfortable with being uncomfortable.

VERONICA VERED is completing her LLB at Trinity College in Dublin after graduating from the University of Toronto in 2016. She is certified by the Canadian Institute of Conflict Resolution at St. Paul's University, has served as a board director for the Jane Goodall Institute of Canada, and is a SheEO activator.

VICKIE SULLIVAN

I **USED TO HAVE** a reputation for being "difficult." My father, the hardscrabble "my way or the highway" type, didn't appreciate hearing my opinion (especially when it differed from his). In his house, girls were seen but not heard. Speaking up was tempting fate, defying "death by dad." Our verbal combat was remembered (and discussed) at his funeral.

What we had in common: our penchant to celebrate. Luxuries were simple back then, so my summer birthday featured grilled homemade hamburgers and ice-cold watermelon in the backyard. For one day, the old man gave me a break. And I honoured the truce by not starting an argument.

On my own after college, birthdays took on a whole new level. This first photo is me celebrating my twenty-fifth. Single and struggling financially, I saved every cent for months for this first limo ride to lunch with a few co-workers. My boss's response: You do know how to do it up. What I thought but didn't say: If I don't celebrate me, who will? No one knew that lunch party was an act of rebellion. It was me saying to the world, "For one day, we're doing things my way. Deal with it."

Over the years, other developments took centre stage. I got married almost ten years after this photo, to a man who still loves my strong-mindedness in all its glory. From him I learned that "my way" could expand to include others.

My rebellion against the status quo launched a now-global business from the ground up, without outside help or contacts. The against-all-odds results made me "controversial" and set new standards in a male-dominated industry. Dad was dumbfounded (and proud) that people actually pay what he made in a year for my advice. I'll never forget what he said in a quiet moment: "I don't know how you did it, but I know you're good at whatever you do." The ultimate praise from my best critic.

But no matter what was going on, personal holidays—birthdays and wedding anniversaries—became sacred. I took a break and celebrated the journey. I learned that, for one day, the world can wait.

I look back in wonder on what my fearlessness (and naivete) has created. The younger set in my family have watched me grow and achieve on my own terms, turning this rebel into a role model. To them, my stubbornness is the difference between struggle and success.

While I can still raise Cain with the best of them, the focus is different now. I no longer fight for my right to an opinion, but for the greater good. I am an advocate, and I use my fearlessness to make the world a better place.

So every year on my birthday, I remember what happens when we stick to our guns, swing for the fences, and live life "our way." Which is why my birthday wish for everyone is to "celebrate *you*."

VICKIE SULLIVAN is internationally recognized as the top market strategist for thought leaders, professional speakers, and B2B firms. Specializing in brand and message strategies in crowded markets, Sullivan has helped thousands of brilliant, talented people outsmart their competition since 1987. She is a popular speaker throughout the US and Canada on why buyers buy in lucrative markets, and on strategies that make thought leaders stand out.

PERSI

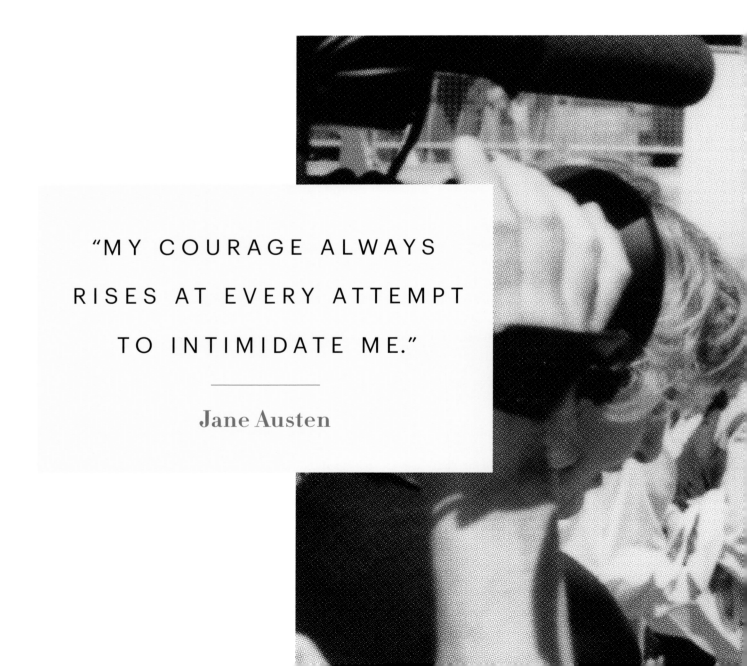

"MY COURAGE ALWAYS
RISES AT EVERY ATTEMPT
TO INTIMIDATE ME."

———

Jane Austen

ST

Magic in the Face of Adversity

THE GREATEST POWER any of us has is the power to choose. We can select our thoughts, actions, and activities. We can decide to think differently about our circumstances, even if we can't control the conditions we find ourselves in. For entrepreneurs, the secret to success is in believing in yourself, keeping supportive and positive people in your circle, and creating a clear vision of what you want, then relentlessly focusing on it. The women in this chapter have chosen to persist in the face of big and small obstacles, finding a way to continue on—sometimes merely by placing one foot in front of the other.

Though my standard setting is "sunny," some days it takes more effort to radiate that sunshine. I remember reading an inspiring little slip of a book called *The Magic of Believing*, just at a time when I needed it. Claude Bristol, a hard-nosed journalist who spent time as a police reporter and served in WWI, wrote it in 1948 to help returning veterans acclimate to civilian life. Hollywood stars like Phyllis Diller and Liberace credited much of their success to the ideas outlined in those pages. (Liberace once said that if he were stranded on a desert island, the two things he'd take with him were his piano and *The Magic of Believing*.) While a bit antiquated and even possibly alienating for some modern readers, it's a nice reminder of the power we have to frame any situation in a positive light.

Since 2015, I've conducted several national studies on women entrepreneurs. It's always fun to spend time talking with my tribe about business, risk, innovation, and, most recently, export as I travel across the country, and I've noticed an interesting pattern. When thinking about how to proceed, many women entrepreneurs ask the same simple question: "What's the worst thing that can happen?"

Seven little words strung together have helped many achieve great things. By staring plainly at the potentially disastrous outcomes, the worst-case scenarios, these entrepreneurs can bring on a sense of calm, and find a positive way forward in the face of what can or will happen—even if the outcome might be terrible. Rather than stick their heads in the sand and let fear overtake the situation, they've used some of the magic of believing to keep going.

There is no substitute for courage and no easy way to be brave, but believing in yourself is a sure way to counter the effects of doubt. Each of the women profiled here are resolute in their efforts to continue on.

JANICE

VICTORIA PELLETIER

T'S DIFFICULT TO choose the photos that best demonstrate the transformative journey I have taken. Culling through my childhood pictures, there was the nerdy girl in her glasses and blue eyeshadow, the girl taking her first steps onto the stage for debate, the sporty and active girl who reflects the passions I have today. But then I found one of the earliest photos of myself. It represents some of the darkest moments of my youth, moments that created fear, great pain, and the fearful little girl that I once was.

At first look, those natural curls and that cute dress offer the appearance of normality to the outside world. But my childhood was anything but normal. Hidden behind the feigned smile and the scratched knees were years of abuse and neglect at the hands of my mother. I was born to a troubled teenager, addicted to drugs and alcohol, someone whose biological and foster families set poor examples of family values and loving behaviour. She didn't know how care for someone else—she couldn't even take care of herself.

For the first few years of my life, I was emotionally and physically abused—pushed down stairs, a cigarette in my eye, a lack of basic necessities, and, quite frankly, a lack of love. The last words my biological mother uttered when I was in her care were "come and get her before I kill her."

Thankfully and fortunately, I was adopted, and avoided living a life in the child welfare system. This was the beginning of my transformation.

I am a fighter, even today. I vowed to be bigger and better than where I came from—I was *not* a product of my life experiences.

I had to learn to trust again. To live and to love without being scared of being abused, or, my biggest fear, being rejected. I am a fighter, even today. I vowed to be bigger and better than where I came from—I was *not* a product of my life experiences. This is why I developed my unstoppable attitude and my approach to life with #NoExcuses.

Once naturally quiet and cautious, I pushed myself to become outgoing and to embrace opportunities rather than shy away. I began working at age eleven, and took my first management role at fourteen (Bata Shoes for the win!). I worked full time through university, and bought my first house at nineteen. I became an executive at barely twenty-four, and have built a career on leading significant change and transformation—though it was a leadership path that many struggle to live by, one that challenges the status quo and strives not just for shareholder value but also for doing the right thing. My leadership mission includes being bold and courageous, and communicating with radical candor—all rooted in the desire to see others succeed. This approach has also built a network of friends and colleagues who support me in every challenge I take on. I am grateful for each of them.

In this picture of me today, there is strength, boldness, courage, and relentless drive. Behind those eyes you can see kindness, compassion, and understanding. And those smile lines show that the journey has also come with great joy and laughter—and that I'm ready to share it with all of you.

VICTORIA PELLETIER is a corporate executive with a global Fortune 50 organization. She is an innovative leader and visionary with over two decades of senior level experience. An inspiring and impactful speaker, Pelletier is a trusted voice in her industry and a respected board member for several organizations.

NANCY CHOW

WHEN I WON the public speaking competition in grade 3, I was thrilled. I had shared my story in front of the entire school, and I felt fearless. I knew I had compelling stories to tell. But soon after, I lost the ability to find the right words. I did not have any words to describe what happened to me when he locked the door.

I have since grown up. I have an amazing husband, and two wonderful children. At Ashbury College, in Ottawa, my children soared, and, to my amazement, it also became my community.

A truly unafraid woman brought me to the table at Ashbury Guild, a volunteer parent's organization. She pulled up a chair and sat next to me until I could find my words again. She supported me until my own voice was able to facilitate others around that same table. Phenomenal women have the strength to truly empower others. They know that it is a journey that takes resiliency.

Back on stage in a school gym, looking out at four hundred people, my fearless self returned. As the new president of Ashbury Guild, I joyfully thanked my friends, my community.

Now, every month, I organize time for women to come and sit around a table, where it is easy to pull up another chair. We share stories—about work, life, anything. But, most importantly, we listen. And embrace all words.

Born in Ottawa and raised in Whitby, Ontario, NANCY CHOW has always pursued her passion for elevating others. Since receiving her bachelor of concurrent education from Queen's University, Chow has used her teaching expertise to foster learning at all educational and social levels.

ANITA AGRAWAL

FEW PEOPLE WOULD find it hard to believe that I was exceptionally shy and quiet as a child, and that I spent most of my time alone. Growing up as a young Indo-Canadian girl in the mostly Caucasian Calgary of the 1980s was often difficult and isolating, not only because was I shy, but also because I had to deal with the unconscious bias of my peers. I was often excluded from sleepovers, hangouts, sports, and other group activities, which exacerbated my loneliness.

In fifth grade, I started going to a more racially diverse school, and that switch helped me find ways to let my personality shine. I've learned over time that there are always both external and internal factors that help shape who we are. The subtle racism I experienced at a young age was not the only factor that determined my personality, but I became stuck in behaviours I developed in response to those external factors: I grew shy, avoided new things, didn't speak up when I wanted to. Sometimes we get set in certain patterns, and ultimately limit ourselves in our ability to achieve the things we are really capable of.

The new school brought about an opportunity for me to do things differently, to really "go out there." Testing out this new personality—without worrying about what my peers thought of me—allowed me to change and grow; I became outgoing, I played sports daily, I ended up doing art projects and becoming student council co-president—all things I had never before

As women, we are socialized to strive to accommodate and to put other people's needs ahead of our own. It took me a long time to realize that we aren't obligated to do this.

thought I could do or be part of. That boost of confidence, the ability to change who I had been before: that was what has propelled me to achieve everything I've done in my life.

Discovering that I enjoy building community and working with others has been a lifelong process for me. I enjoy making a difference and working with like-minded people toward a common goal. When we are younger, we are so reliant on the opinion of others; as women, we are socialized to strive to accommodate and to put other people's needs ahead of our own. It took me a long time to realize that we aren't obligated to do this. As well-meaning and well-intentioned as our friends and family can be, sometimes they can hold us back from achieving our full potential. This limits us from seeking out people or communities who share our same vision, and want to build something together.

In the years since I was that shy, quiet girl, I've had the privilege to run a business with my mom; chair several not-for-profit organizations in different disciplines; speak out on social justice issues on TV and in newspapers; create and exhibit my art locally and internationally; travel to over thirty-five countries; participate in trade missions around the world; write; run

for federal, provincial, and local politics; and teach postgraduate students. Living an authentic life and being true to one's passions takes time—but I encourage you to try new things, and to break out of the personal behaviour patterns that might be holding you back.

———————————

ANITA AGRAWAL is CEO of Best Bargains Jewellery and a professor in the Faculty of Business at Centennial College. She is a former president of the Organization of Women in International Trade (OWIT), Toronto Chapter; in 2010 Agrawal was named to the Profit W100 list, and in 2012 she was named Ontario Women Exporter of the Year by OWIT.

JEANETTE SOUTHWOOD

I REMEMBER A MOMENT when I was on the beach with my grandfather in South Africa, the country where I was born. At the time, South Africa was under apartheid, a system of institutionalized racism. My family was classified as "coloured," a mix of black and white. Because of that, the beach where we were standing was a "coloured" beach, designated as such because of its unfavourable characteristics, including a strong undertow and a location bordering shark-infested waters.

Of course, I did not know that at the time. But not long after, I had my first experience of apartheid as a young child: travelling on a bus where there were no available seats in the non-white section, I went to sit in an empty seat in the white section. The conductor came to tell me that I could not sit there and needed to go back to the non-white section, where my babysitter was standing with her friends. I went back briefly—then snuck back to the empty seat in the white section. The conductor came back, and this time took me

back to my babysitter, telling all of us that if I went back to sit in the white section, we would all be in trouble.

Because of apartheid, my grandfather could not become an engineer, despite being a talented student and employee. So while my sisters and I were still young, my parents—concerned for our future and our safety—emigrated to Canada, a country that welcomed us.

This photo of me today is one that would have been completely unbelievable years ago to someone who was looking at that young girl on a shark-infested coloured beach, or to that child on the bus being told she could not sit in an empty seat because of her colour. My path was not an easy one. Engineering is a male-dominated profession. I'm sure that many of you reading this have seen the research that describes some of the success factors for young women in engineering: the belief of family, peer support, role models, men as allies, an excellent education, and the forging of bonds with social, professional, and technical networks. For myself—a young woman of colour who was a first-generation Canadian, first-generation university student, and first-generation engineer—if it was not for my wonderful teachers, professors, colleagues, friends, and family members, I would not have appeared in such a photo.

An award-winning engineer, JEANETTE SOUTHWOOD is VP, corporate affairs and strategic partnerships, at Engineers Canada, the national organization of the twelve regulators licensing Canada's more than 300,000 engineers. Previously, Southwood led the Canadian urban development and infrastructure sector and the global sustainable cities teams at an international consulting firm.

BRITTANY FORSYTH

I GREW UP VERY lucky to have the best family and friends. It was a happy life, to say the least. Every day was an adventure, full of new experiences and new memories. I was never afraid to take a chance, or to fail. It was a life full of bumps, scrapes, and a few tears.

But over the years, life got harder, and the reality of a new kind of life and its difficulties set in. This new existence included life and death, successes and epic failures, and many more memories. In those years, it felt as though I was losing a little piece of me, daily. And it was all in the search of becoming the best leader, best executive, and best friend I could be.

I strived to be the best to everyone, and in that striving I forgot to be the best to myself. But as you can see by the massive smile on my face in this later picture, I found that ability again. Just a little piece, each day—through remembering that there is beauty in the hard moments. And in the growth that comes from them. I stand here today as an imperfect human, doing her best to be herself.

BRITTANY FORSYTH is an energetic and passionate individual who leads the human relations function as chief talent officer at Shopify, one of Ottawa's fastest growing tech companies. Talent, culture, systems, growth, development, and technology are her passions. Over the years, her role has changed often, but her focus has always remained the same: finding and empowering the right people while designing an environment focused on solving tough problems.

BOBBIE LAPORTE

THE PHOTO ON the next set of pages is me as a young girl—maybe five or six years old—on my new bike at Christmas. It looks like a happy time, but my memory of my early childhood was anything but happy.

I was an only child, spoiled, the centre of attention and the focus of my parents' world. When I was three, my mother was diagnosed with leukemia. I hardly remember her. I do remember my dad being full of love and life, yet grieving for all of us and the loss of his beautiful young bride at the age of thirty-five. I was five years old when she died.

Life after that was challenging. My relationship with my stepmother was dark and difficult. I learned early on that little girls should be seen and not heard. Our home was based on structure and discipline; I saw little praise and even less love. School and study became my refuge; I buried myself in books and learning. I was shy and introverted, lacking confidence, unsure. I kept to myself, with few friends and outside interests. I honestly don't even remember riding that new bike at Christmas.

College and my early career days were focused on achievement and proving myself. I enjoyed success, but I always felt like it wasn't real, that I would be found out, that it wouldn't last. Through my thirties and forties life—and work—went on, but I always felt that there was something missing.

I found that something in October 2003.

Two years earlier I had run my first marathon. I was tired of being out of shape, spending endless hours in the start-up I was running, and looking for a *big* challenge—for me, the consummate non-athlete.

A friend suggested I train for a short-distance triathlon, so I did. Then someone suggested I train for an Ironman triathlon. That's 140.6 human-powered miles: a 2.4-mile open water swim and a 122-mile bike ride, followed by a marathon (26.2 miles of running). My initial thought was: *are you kidding?*

But the more I thought about the sheer immensity of the challenge, the more seriously I considered it. Little did I know I was signing up for nine months of pain and suffering, intense learning about my capabilities and vulnerabilities, and being immersed 24/7 in a self-discovery process that was totally transformational. I still doubted ("I am *never* going to finish this race"), but when race day came and I crossed the finish line, I experienced pure joy, and pure gratitude for what I was able to achieve. I was finally able to believe in myself.

I have now completed six Ironman-distance triathlons and countless others. I don't consider myself a role model of any kind, but I have been

When race day came and I crossed the finish line, I experienced pure joy, and pure gratitude for what I was able to achieve. I was finally able to believe in myself.

successful in using the knowledge, insight, and experience I gained from my training and racing to help other leaders see what is truly possible for them. And every day, when I face a new problem or challenge, I say: "I can do this. I am an Ironman."

My current racing bike has seen me through thousands of miles of training and countless races, and has been my guide through the highs and lows of my life as an endurance athlete. I wish I could ride it to my past and tell the little girl on her Christmas bike that it will all be fine. She will learn to love herself; she will do big things. And she will help others achieve beyond their expectations, too.

BOBBIE LAPORTE is CEO of Bobbie LaPorte & Associates, a consultancy providing leadership development services to Fortune 500 companies, global organizations, and promising start-ups. LaPorte has served in CXO roles in Fortune 50 companies and healthcare technology start-ups. She has an MBA from Harvard and a master's in positive leadership from IE in Madrid.

STEPHANIE RICHARDSON

WHEN I SEE myself as a young girl, I smile. I think of how happy I was. How loved and cherished I was. I felt that the world was a beautiful and safe place. I had a sense of belonging. I felt like I was a part of a community: family, friends and neighbours.

No matter where life took me, I had this sense of love and joy. By no means was it because things were always perfect. Rather, it was that when things weren't, I felt that they would work out. That the bumps would pass.

In the spring of 2010, I turned forty. I felt blessed. I had a wonderful husband and two beautiful daughters that I loved beyond words. I had a great family, friends, and community. I still felt the joy that I had felt all those years ago.

That fall, my life became a nightmare. One of my most cherished loved ones, my beautiful youngest daughter, died.

My world went from being beautiful to becoming a very dark and scary place. There is no way to describe the sadness I felt or the pain that I now carry in my soul. I did not recognize myself, in spirit or in the mirror. I felt despair and impending doom all the time. There was no peace and there was no joy.

I was recently shown a picture of myself that was taken not long ago. I am standing between two incredible women. I felt loved and supported enough

to venture back into the world. My family, my friends, and my community were fierce with their love and support. They made sure I got back to a place of feeling not only that I was ok, but also that I was loved, cherished, and blessed.

I recognized myself for the first time in a very long while.

Life is not perfect. There will be more bumps. But there is joy in the world.

STEPHANIE RICHARDSON is a mental health champion and a founding member of #DIFD—a youth-driven initiative focused on raising awareness and inspiring conversations about youth mental health. She is also a mother, the wife of Luke Richardson, and a committed volunteer who is interested in making a difference.

JENNIFER HARPER

THIS IS THE story of how Cheekbone started. Because without my sobriety, it would not exist.

This is also the story of a woman. She is forty years old, married with a couple of children, and she is Ojibwe Canadian. She works full time, and if you met her ten years ago, you would think she had everything she could want. A house, a nice car, family, friends, and a good job.

The problem was her past, her family's past. She had pain, and she had no idea that it was likely rooted in the suffering some of her family had experienced. She had a grandmother who was a residential school survivor, which basically means she made it out, she didn't die at the school. But that grandmother left the system with scars... numerous scars, physical and emotional. She was taken from the family without consent; she was put in a school system and abused, repeatedly. If she tried to speak Ojibwe she would be physically punished.

The grandmother went on to have eight children. They all lived in a very small house in Northern Ontario, with no electricity and no running water. While the setting was beautiful, on a lake, in an area untouched by the hustle and bustle of big cities, the scars ran deep. The grandmother abused alcohol to mask the childhood pain. She raised her children without a sense of what a loving parent meant. Because she was taken from the family at such a young age, she never learned how to love, or what love was. Even as a young adult, there was no therapy to re-teach her.

The grandmother's son—the father of the woman this story is about—was the second oldest and had to help with his younger siblings and pick up the pieces when his parents would disappear for days. The father left the reserve, tried going to college, tried living in the big city. He met a woman and had a child, and that child was the woman I know. This woman's father didn't want to be in the city; he wanted to be close to nature, close to home, and close to others like him. He too was unhappy, and after watching his parents turn to alcohol, he did the same thing. And he left his child and her mother.

The father had a sporadic relationship with his oldest child. He had other children with other women and at times he abandoned them as well. His children were now experiencing the same things their grandmother, the residential school survivor, experienced. They lacked love, they lacked direction, and they lacked one or both of their parents.

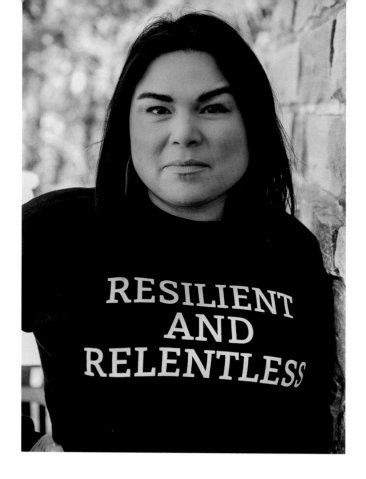

So this woman left her father and lived with her mother, growing up with no connection to her Ojibwe heritage. She was encouraged at times to explore it, but she struggled with identity. She would lie, and not say that she was Ojibwe. She had heard all the jokes and stereotypes, and so she was embarrassed. She was embarrassed by the history of her family and by her father's continuing battle with alcohol.

When she was in her teens, living without any professional or spiritual help, her pain and lack of self-identity was too much. She too turned to alcohol. It suppressed her feelings of worthlessness, of being abandoned by her father; it helped her deal with her loneliness. She was raised poor by a single mother, and learned to drink her pain away. She put herself in vulnerable situations, always involving alcohol; she was raped in her teens, and again in her twenties. She continued to drink. She got married, but into her thirties she continued to drink. Her marriage was rocky at times, and she still continued to drink. It caused problems—a domestic altercation got

I believe, as has been said many times, that what didn't kill me has only made me stronger.

out of control, and the police were involved. She sat in a courtroom with her husband the next day and listened to a judge tell her how alcohol was clearly a problem.

That was in 2009. In 2010, she finally sought help and admitted that alcohol was a problem. This woman entered a five-week treatment program and completed it. She had a few relapses along the way, and after one last drinking episode that could have had drastic consequences, she quit for good.

I am happy to say that I have been sober since November 26, 2014, and, yes, I have been speaking about me. But that woman no longer exists. I have overcome alcoholism and I feel great about who I am. I needed to quit: the narrative about me, about my people, that narrative had to change. After getting sober, I realized I wanted to be a part of the solution and alter the course of my family. I believe, as has been said many times, that what didn't kill me has only made me stronger.

JENNIFER HARPER is the founder and CEO of Cheekbone Beauty Cosmetics Inc. She developed Cheekbone to create a brand for real people, that was made in Canada, not tested on animals, and gave back to the First Nations community. In 2017, Harper was awarded the Social Enterprise Award by Women in Niagara Council and the Greater Niagara Chamber of Commerce.

JACKIE KING

LOOK AT THE little girl on the next page and see confidence. Someone who can pull off a Wonder Woman cape and a power pose that says to the world: "I got this." She is an inspiration.

But I know this girl. I know how shy she is. I know how much she has had to overcome, and how hard she had to work to see the positive in every experience. And I know that at times she puts on her superhero cape to convince herself—as much as to convince the world—that she really has "got this."

I was almost five when I first moved to Canada from Ireland. To help me make friends, my parents enrolled me in a summer program that culminated in a show. It was my first on-stage performance, and I had one line: "If I was a bear, I'd sit in a chair and comb my hair." How hard could that be? But all I remember is being on stage, starting my line, and then running off, crying. I was mortified.

That feeling stuck with me. The fear of speaking in front of a crowd. Or walking into a room where I didn't know anyone. But here's the thing: I didn't actually die of embarrassment. And I wanted to experience as much as I could, even then. So I decided that being shy was not going to work for me.

Through sheer will, I forced myself into situations where I had to face my fear. And today, I'm still conquering that fear, speaking at global conferences in front of hundreds of people. And when I tell people I'm shy, they don't believe me.

Like many, I've faced adversity in my life. The details don't matter, but the effects are the same: something happens that has the potential to knock you down and make you give up. But from an early age, I decided that, no matter what happened, I would not be a victim. I would never give up when there were more important things at stake. And I would try to focus on the lessons of life and on the positive. For me that came down to two things: perspective and perseverance.

When my children were five and seven, I unexpectedly became a single mother. I went back to school full time, and waited tables to make ends meet. I was afraid I couldn't possibly support two children, and go to school—and, and, and... It was tough, and at times overwhelming. I thought about putting off school, but then I thought about what example that would set for my kids.

From an early age, I decided that, no matter what happened, I would not be a victim. I would never give up when there were more important things at stake.

I made a plan. I set goals. Sometimes, those goals were short term. "I just have to make it through today." "I just have to make it to next payday." "I just have to get through this semester." There were times when I wasn't sure I could do it. But I had two little people counting on me, so I put on a smile and my Wonder Woman cape to convince my kids that "mom's got this." It made our life seem like an adventure, and in the process I convinced myself.

With each goal, I became stronger, more determined, and more confident. I graduated with honours, got a job as an intern at an international firm, and accelerated through the ranks to executive leadership. Then I became COO of Canada's largest and most influential business association. Along the way, I have raised two amazing, happy, kind people who are at the core of our strong and growing family.

I'm still shy. But it hasn't stopped me from leading. Instead of being out front, I build up the team around me. I encourage them to think big, take chances, and embrace the lessons of failure. In other words, I try to inspire them to be fearless, and to imagine what's possible.

———————

JACKIE KING is an entrepreneurial, forward-thinking business leader with a twenty-year track record of performance in turnaround and high-paced organizations. She is known for being a visionary strategist, and respected as a proponent of empowerment and accountability.

BLOOM

"YOU DON'T HAVE TO
DEPEND ON SOMEONE
TELLING YOU
WHO YOU ARE."

Beyoncé Knowles

From Small Seed to Dazzling Brilliance

I'M A NOTICER. I've always been one. My gaze will often land on lovely things because beauty inspires me. It could be fabrics, flowers, vistas, art, architecture—I take it all in. Music, in particular, is everything to me. I can listen to a song on repeat forever. Discovering new music and seeing live shows is my fuel. I spent decades in the music industry and it was so satisfying. To be able to meet incredible creators and be surrounded by up-and-coming and top talent has continued to inspire me. I saw firsthand the hard work, determination, and commitment to the craft that success demanded of artists as they bloomed into stars.

Music is number one for me, but I am also an avid reader. Because of my intense curiosity, everything interests me. I coined a phrase to describe how I read: "Broadly and Oddly." An old copy of *Popular Science* magazine could easily be followed by *The Economist, Vanity Fair,* and the latest best-selling biography as I zip through the stack. It's the same thing with music: from Patsy Cline to Chet Baker to Prince, I love many genres. Reading is a favourite pastime and books and music are constant companions. No trip is complete without a long list of things to consume and discover.

My mother loves to read, but she also loves orchids, which is why I do, too. Delicate and fickle, these ancient plants have been around since the age of dinosaurs, making them some of the first flowering plants on earth. There are more than thirty thousand different species of orchid, and each variety has an almost magical beauty and allure.

Musicians and authors are compelled to create. They hear the music, or know the story they need to share. They don't wait to be invited to do so. It's the same thing with a flowering orchid. It doesn't think about competing with the flower next to it. It doesn't ask permission to grow. Or wait to be invited to bloom. It blooms. Each of the women profiled here have given themselves permission to use their voice and their talents to stand in their full power, to step out of their comfort zones, and to sprout, develop, and bloom.

JANICE

LISA KIMMEL

THE PICTURES IN this story illustrate how I got comfortable—with being uncomfortable.

Public speaking—for many, it incites jitters. For me, it used to incite absolute terror, as you can see in this photo, taken when I was about twelve or thirteen. I can't remember what I was called upon to speak about, but I do remember the fear, vividly. My body would shake. My voice would crack. I'd even end up with blotches all over my face. Chalk it up to my introvert status, shying away from the spotlight, whatever the reason—I absolutely hated speaking up.

On my old report cards, my teachers would often say I was diligent, bright—but I needed to contribute more in class. My best friend frequently tells the story of how I "ordered" her to call for pizza delivery when we were teenagers because I was too scared even to do that. And when I when I was at Humber College earning my PR certificate, just thinking about presenting in front of the class would make me feel sick.

But today, on any given week, in any given city, you'll find me engaged in some form of public speaking. Whether it's for a pitch to a client, a town hall in front of employees, or a keynote speech at an event, I'm often in front of a crowd. In fact, I've even had people tell me how comfortable I look presenting, and ask me for tips on how to boost their own comfort levels in front of a group.

So . . . what changed?

I realized that the only way to be successful in my role was to get comfortable with being uncomfortable.

Don't get me wrong: while I've certainly become used to public speaking—and I purposely make every effort to do it—it still doesn't feel natural. But eventually I realized that the only way to be successful in my role was to get comfortable with being uncomfortable. That meant I simply had to overcome my fear of public speaking in order to advance in my career and be the leader I always wanted to be. Because, let's face it: it's pretty hard to lead a team, be the "face" of a company, or otherwise be an influencer if you can't or won't put yourself out there.

I believe in this approach so strongly that I've even told my kids, Sam and Chloe, that every day they should proactively seek out something that makes them uncomfortable—whether it's volunteering for an assignment, learning a skill, or meeting someone new. Ask questions instead of fearing the unknown. Curb defeatist thinking, which can erode your self-confidence. Ask for feedback from people who can help you understand what you need to improve.

And don't let labels like "introvert" or "shy" define what you can do.

LISA KIMMEL oversees Edelman's Canadian and Latin American operations and is chair of its Global Women's Equality Network (GWEN). She is one of the WXN Top 100 Most Powerful Women in Canada and is a recipient of the *Financial Times* & HERoes Female Champion of Women in Business and a YWCA Toronto Women of Distinction award.

ZAINAB MUSE

GROWING UP, I suffered severely from stage fright. I always thought it was because I was an imposter. "Why was I chosen to stand in front of a microphone facing a crowd?" I'd think. "What do I have to say?" And "Why does this crowd have to listen to me?"

It was such an issue that, when I was in boarding school in Nigeria, my home country, my stage fright was a big part of being rejected for a prefectship. I remember distinctly being told, "Zainab, we were considering you for the highest prefectship role. You're a very brilliant girl and you're likeable, but you're extremely shy. We want someone that can represent the school confidently on whatever stage they're invited to."

I was crushed. But it didn't affect me right away, not in the way I had hoped. Not until I moved to Canada. One day, I was reading a young adult novel called *The Sky Is Everywhere*, by Jandy Nelson. In my first year of university, reading fiction was my escape, since I was missing home very deeply. In this book, the protagonist experiences a personal growth journey, one that built her confidence. There's a sentence in the book I will never forget, because it altered my perception of myself. It read something like, "You're the protagonist of your own story; no one can tell it better than you."

This became the mantra I chose to live by—and, in fact, I began to own my story, to aspire for the impossible and lead an extraordinary life. Because, after all, I was the author of my journey and no one could design my life

> # It was never the crowd I feared, it was not being accepted. And when I completely embraced who I was and owned my journey, it no longer mattered what anyone else thought.

better than I could. This understanding translated into how I addressed people on and off stage.

A lot has transpired in the nine years since I first read that book. In 2019, I was awarded the title of Entrepreneur of the Year by Women in Communications and Technology, and when I got on stage to tell my story and accept the award, it all came full circle for me.

I love the work I do and the conviction I have that influences my mission as an entrepreneur. And now, when I stand on stage, I not only believe that my story is worth sharing, I also know that I have something to say—something that is unique to me—and that, because of this, I deserve a place on that stage, mic in hand, addressing the crowd. I now realize that in all those years of being afraid, it was never the crowd I feared, it was not being accepted. And when I completely embraced who I was and owned my journey, it no longer mattered what anyone else thought. In essence, I no longer had to hustle for anyone else's acceptance. All I needed was to accept myself—wholly and unconditionally.

—————

ZAINAB MUSE is an award-winning entrepreneur, strategist, process designer, interactive digital media expert, and filmmaker. She is the founder and CEO of Wingd Inc. and Creatorland.

RUTA AIDIS

I N THIS FIRST picture, I'm about two years old. I like this photo for several reasons, but mainly because I am enjoying myself, and look prepared to take on anything that comes my way. My bathing suit is obviously too small—a detail that does not deter my two-year-old self in the slightest way. I keep the big picture in mind. I look directly at the camera and show no signs of being self-conscious or shy. I'm also not striking a pose or giving a practiced "cute" smile. I am genuine, sincere, and engaged. Delightfully inquisitive, and eager and ready to see what comes next.

This photo was taken at a time when I think my true self showed through, and I was unrestrained by social norms. But, slowly, that changed. A few years later, while visiting my father's workplace, I was labelled "shy," and I continued to be perceived as shy in public for a long time afterward. But I know that when I saw something happen that I thought was wrong, I spoke up and acted. In elementary school, after I learned about the health dangers of smoking, I smelled smoke coming from the school's teacher's lounge and I decided to do something about it. On my own, I made little plaques about the health risks, took them to the principal's office and insisted they be placed in the teacher's lounge. I even snuck by at the next opportunity to make sure they were really hanging on the walls.

In adolescence, I bent to the increasing peer pressure and veered away from listening to my inner voice for guidance, instead looking for direction from magazines, which in those days focused squarely on improving your outer appearance to be the perfect girl. I followed their beauty tips, fretting over keeping my nails polished and unchipped and mastering eyebrow plucking, even though my eyebrows were so light coloured they were literally invisible. I learned to second-guess myself, and to value my looks over my ideas.

Thankfully, during my college years that little girl inside started regaining her voice. Once again, I found the conviction to address injustices, especially when it came to equal rights for women. I spoke out, organizing campaigns, street theatre, and demonstrations.

Now, in my fifties, activism is embedded in my work and in all aspects of my life. When confronted by injustices, I go out on a limb to raise awareness, sometimes even risking my job in the process. I've developed metrics, diagnostics, case studies, research, and reports to reach broader audiences—especially decision makers—and educated them about the need and benefits of systematically working toward gender equality.

Several years ago, I felt drained and disheartened at the slow place of change, and the frequent backlashes against gender equality. I came across this old photo of my two-year-old self, and had it enlarged and framed as a reminder to reconnect with that energy inside. Now, when I feel daunted, that little girl within is there to reinvigorate me, and to guide my choices in following through with actions that truly feel right.

———————

DR. RUTA AIDIS is the founder of ACG Inc, a research director at Gender Metrics, and a senior fellow at George Mason University. Aidis has authored over fifty publications and spearheaded the development of innovative comparative gendered metrics and diagnostic tools, and is a leading global expert in women's economic empowerment, entrepreneurship, innovation, public policy, and economic development.

HELEN HIRSH SPENCE

N THIS FIRST picture, I am about six or seven, and my brother and I are heading up Mt. Washington in New Hampshire on the cog railway. It took a bit of courage to head up there on our own and, quite frankly, I can't understand why our parents weren't with us. This would have been the 1950s, and "stranger danger" wasn't yet taught to children.

This was one of my first mountain ascents and it set the stage for my later love of trekking in the Himalayas, and for climbing some of the world's highest peaks, like Kilimanjaro.

In the early 1960s, when I was about thirteen, I was sent abroad to learn French in Switzerland, while most of my peers were being sent away to summer camp. I was on my own, didn't know what awaited me. I was too young to be really scared but I was definitely anxious. I felt awkward, out of my depth. It was the '60s and I was acutely aware that straight, long hair parted in the middle was fashionable, but my hair was very curly and short. It was almost as if my hair defined me as an outsider. I was never in tune with the norm. My mother, who wouldn't let me grow it as she thought it would be too unmanageable, insisted that it was good to be different; she was as strong willed as I eventually became, and she didn't understand how desperately teens want conformity.

But these lessons—independence, being comfortable on my own—helped me take atypical paths later in my life. I fear less now, because I learned as a

young girl to move out of my comfort zone. In fact, even today, at least once a year I make a point of challenging myself and deliberately undertaking something that is uncomfortable, just to ensure that I maintain perspective and continue to appreciate the wonderful life I have.

The most frightening and yet most exciting experience of my recent life has been to become a social entrepreneur in my late sixties. Every day I find myself totally outside of my comfort zone. Everything I am doing as a start-up is new to me. While I'm registering my business, setting up a website, or familiarizing myself with all types of social media, I am always finding myself in a state of constant, positive stress and anxiety about this new world I have entered.

My adult children are now my cheerleaders, my husband has always been a rock, and my grandchildren keep me grounded and conscious of how precious life is in the present. My family is immensely supportive, and I derive courage from them.

On a daily basis, I am pushing my personal boundaries. I refuse to buy into the bias against older adults, the one that dictates an expiry date on

productivity. I am older, but I am just as capable, creative, and innovative as I was years ago. I am learning, meeting new people, finding my way in a world that is entirely unlike the one I knew. It is invigorating and thrilling. I feel alive, and I have purpose.

After an extensive career as an educational leader, HELEN HIRSH SPENCE has launched her most recent entrepreneurial venture, Top Sixty over Sixty. This social enterprise works with businesses and organizations to transform multigenerational workforces into productive, intergenerational teams. It advocates for a more inclusive and age-diverse workplace.

JAN FROLIC

I'M HAPPY. I'VE always been happy and I've always been comfortable being me, but I didn't realize it until I saw these pictures. There is something soothing about seeing how similar I am now to who I was as a child. Stupid hats, big glasses, and a big smile seem to have been my thing right from the beginning.

It is so much more obvious that I am exactly the "me" I am supposed to be, and that there has been a natural evolution of my authentic self over the past half-century. Being comfortable in my skin from an early age has allowed me to really know and understand who I am. That self-awareness has created closer connections, and better empathy and compassion for others. My personal and professional life has been a continual build of fabulous people and experiences. It's nice to see that this comfort started early, and it explains why I have such deep and vast stories and relationships in my life.

Looking at these pictures has given me the freedom to just relax into the future and continue to live the best life I can, having the most fun I can and creating the most impact I can. Live fiercely, love deeply, and, apparently, know your style.

JAN FROLIC is a serial entrepreneur with a passion for advocacy and inclusion. She is senior VP, global engagement, at Women of Influence Worldwide Inc., a global organization that works for the advancement of women in the workplace. Frolic has three children and a life full of love surrounded by the very best people.

FRANÇOISE GAGNON

THIS PHOTO PORTRAYS my true self. Although it's undated, in it I am about two years old. I was very shy as a child, and disliked being the centre of attention. Even in this familiar surrounding, being photographed by family, I hid behind a rubber tree. This photo goes a long way in revealing who I was and who I am: someone who is inherently introverted. I grew up in a rural setting, playing in the forest that surrounded our house. There was nothing girly about me: no Barbies, no pretty dresses, I didn't even like to comb my hair! My free time was spent with neighbourhood kids, boys and girls, climbing trees, wading through creeks, and playing in the farmers' fields next door. We always had pet rabbits and dogs, and I campaigned fruitlessly to get a horse.

Television was strictly regulated in our house. There was one hour of TV time on Sunday for the *The Wonderful World of Disney* or *Quelle famille!*, and exceptions were made for any National Geographic special. I entertained myself by reading everything I could get my hands on, including Asterix, Tintin, *Comtesse de Ségur*, and every issue of *National Geographic* as soon as it arrived in our home.

I always did well in school, yet I doubt anyone would remember me from back then. I did not run for student council, did not play team sports, and did not hang out with the cool kids.

To thine own self be true—nothing much has changed! Once I graduated from university and entered the job market, the professional world was a

seismic shift. Back in school, I never had to raise my hand, I hid in the shadows, and my performance was measured through exams. In my career, hiding in the wings did not work; I was just overlooked or underestimated. When I was reluctant to speak up, others were happy to step in and fill the void.

To progress, I had to step out of my comfort zone. I had to network, and build relationships to create opportunities to compete and succeed. It was work, but it paid off. I took on management responsibilities, gained seniority, and earned a reputation as someone who got things done.

To progress, I had to step out of my comfort zone. I had to network, and build relationships to create opportunities to compete and succeed.

Today, I am the CEO of ADGA, a company that operates in the fields of defence, security, space, and information technology. I lead a team of seven hundred, and I am the only female owner of a Canadian company in these domains. The work we do matters to our economy, and to our national security.

Since coming into this role, I have made it my mission to be someone who raises up other women, to help them secure their place in our industry. I support the women who work for our companies with a professional development program, and I support the broader community of women through scholarships in STEM. I am moving the needle forward in our industry by leading a working group on diversity and inclusion with industry and government representation.

I feel empowered in my role, but I remain shy by nature, and still quite introverted. I am re-energized in a rural setting, walking through the woods with our two dogs. My personal time is spent with my husband, family, and close friends. I may lead a company, but I am still "that girl."

FRANÇOISE GAGNON, ICD, D., is the CEO of ADGA Group, Presidia Security Consulting, and Extravision Security Technologies. As one of a handful of female executives within the defence, security, and technology sector in Canada, Françoise is a champion of diversity and balance in the workplace. In 2018, Gagnon was named one of Canada's Most Powerful Women by the Women's Executive Network.

CATHERINE CANO

WHEN I WAS young, even as a toddler, I was solid on my feet, confident, ready to take on the world. Yes, I might have been a bit shy, but I was attentive. Back then, I loved being in the middle of a room, listening to the conversations around me. I still do!

Today, three things guide my decisions at the professional level: passion for the mission, focus on public service and the usefulness of the mandate, and a determination to work in a collaborative and respectful environment. My desire to discover my country; to learn to speak English; and to listen, learn, and understand others has resulted in my standing—and standing tall—for what I believe in.

CATHERINE CANO is an award-winning leader. A change agent, she is sought after to transform and modernize national, international, and multilateral organizations. She has been at the helm of media networks, run public and private companies, and driven change management through the digital and technology evolution. An expert on political processes, Cano has been an advocate of public policies supporting democracy and human rights. She is recognized for her innovation and work on democratic literacy and education. Cano was chosen to become the administratrice (COO) of the Organisation Internationale de la Francophonie, and was the first woman to do so in fifty years.

LAURA PECK

ALL OF MY life I wanted a career in which I could use whatever talents I have to achieve something, and to help other people. The picture on the next page, with me in front of the Christmas tree, was taken in my family home in Sydney Mines, Cape Breton. Looking at that rocking horse reminds me that my earliest memories were always of going forward. My father, Bernard Peck, was a well-known horse trainer and driver throughout the Maritimes, so horses were a big part of my life. My most profound influences during my early years, however, were the strong women in my family—starting with my mother, Grace Howley Peck.

I am a third-generation career woman whose ambitions were always to go away to university, and I knew that the economic reality of Cape Breton meant I would have a career away from home. As several of my relatives have said to me over the years, "Laura had her bags packed by the time she was eleven." Whether I was working in the family grocery store or at a summer job in broadcasting, I sensed it was my journey to use whatever talents I had to communicate and to connect with every different kind of person I met. And boy, did I!

When I learned I could go to university at the end of grade 11, I realized I was far closer than I had thought to getting on with my life. Later, working as a supply teacher throughout Cape Breton, I found a passion for teaching,

and for helping students and treating them as individuals. I particularly recall with great fondness my time teaching at Eskasoni School with children from the Mi'kmaq First Nations.

I always had an interest in politics, at every level. I loved everything from the policy discussions to campaigning and meeting strangers at the door, and on the street. I didn't entirely realize it at the time, but it turns out that these were skills and character traits that were actually valued! Who knew?

This later photo was taken as I gave the keynote address at a community and economic development conference at Cape Breton University. During the trip back, I was invited to teach a course in strategic communications in the university's MBA program. The experience reminded me of how life

The *Fearless Girl* statue installed in New York City in 2017 has profound meaning for me. It shows not that we are without fear, but that we can "fear less" and still move forward.

comes full circle. I was going back to the island where I grew up, to share with new generations—particularly young women—how to communicate and to navigate the uncertain waters that surround us today.

That opportunity grew out of three decades of working as a communications trainer and consultant, and, prior to that, three years of working as an executive assistant on Canada's Parliament Hill. So much of what has infused my life's journey has been the result of my ongoing fascination with people—and with the power that communication has to overcome life's challenges and roadblocks.

The *Fearless Girl* statue installed in New York City in 2017 has profound meaning for me. It shows not that we are without fear, but that we can "fear less" and still move forward. And, most importantly, keep moving forward. Just like that girl on the rocking horse, so many years ago.

LAURA M. PECK is a leadership communications consultant who has spent over three decades working with political and business leaders to teach them how to achieve their potential as communicators. Her greatest achievements are the young women whom she has mentored at universities, workplaces, and in everyday life.

LEAD

"EACH PERSON MUST LIVE THEIR LIFE AS A MODEL FOR OTHERS."

———

Rosa Parks

How to Be Extraordinary

EXTRAORDINARY PEOPLE are just like everyone else, with one exception: they care deeply about high performance and put much more effort into what they're trying to accomplish than others do. Because of that, they do better for longer periods of time. In his book *High Performance Habits*, Brendon Burchard, the *New York Times* bestselling author, outlines how extraordinary people become extraordinary. He spent twenty years working to understand why some individuals and teams succeed more quickly than others, and sustain that success over the long term. He also wanted to know why some people are miserable as they strive for success, and others are happy on their journey. And, finally, he wanted to know what motivates people to reach for higher levels of success in the first place.

Here's what he found: *anyone* can dramatically increase their results and become a high performer in almost any field or career. How do you do this? You apply a specific set of habits to learn adjacent competencies that bolster your particular expertise. Then you bring all of that forward and use your multiple skill sets to lead others. As a member of the International Women's Forum, I network with exceptional women from around the world, whether it's at the global conferences or in my past role as a director on the Foundation board. The IWF members I meet reflect the best of women's leadership around the world. They all exhibit the high-performance habits of leaders that Burchard identifies: clarity, energy, courage, influence, productivity, and necessity.

Although their stories vary greatly, the women leaders featured in this section all have these attributes in common. They love challenges and know they can overcome adversity. As Burchard writes, too many people avoid any sense of hardship in their lives. They dwell on the idea that they can't handle it, or worry that they'll be judged or rejected, so they let fear win. These women, however, are different. They may have moments of self-doubt, but they believe in themselves and their ability to figure things out.

As I've often said, I will always bet on myself! These women leaders see challenges as an opportunity to grow, and they work to overcome the barriers in place. As a result, they inspire others and are admired by many. As you read their stories, you will see how they live as passionate servant leaders.

JANICE

DEBORAH TRUDEAU

WAS THE ELDEST of twelve children, and I took on a leadership role from the very beginning. It was organic, and with the arrival of each new sibling came more responsibility, more chores, more chaos, and more "fun." Our home was a happy home, with great spirit and lots of laughter. Neighbouring kids were often found at our table—it was entertaining, and our dinners could always be stretched to accommodate a few more.

The photo you'll see of me as a ballerina soldier represents my life back then. Being in charge, paving the way, having the responsibility for my siblings, all while always ensuring the well-being of all those around me.

I continued to warrior on through life with a sense of adventure, determination, and leadership, qualities that have led to a love for business, marketing, and entrepreneurship.

At a young age we were told that—not *if*, but *when*—we went to university, we needed to be prepared to pay our own way. This instilled in all of us a strong work ethic and the importance of financial independence.

After university and some travelling, I began my career in advertising, went on to publish a restaurant guide, and started my own PR/advertising venture (called "Strategie Shannon") by my early twenties. Shortly after marriage and two children, I joined Trudeau Corp., a family business specializing in the design and distribution of kitchenware and tableware products.

It did not take long to recognize the need to develop our own creations and build our own brand, leading to a transformation from general importer

It takes a "warrior spirit" to navigate through life—to seek opportunities, challenge the odds, deal with the curveballs and the unforeseen. The unexpected awaits every day.

to vertically integrated company. I recognized the benefits of innovation, private label, and licensing, and formed our in-house creative department. Influenced by my own children's love for *Sesame Street*, we began our first licensed children's tableware line under Sesame Street for Canada. This expanded to other character licences for brands such as Disney and Mattel, and we pioneered the development of licensed programs and strategic partnerships in Canada, Europe, Eastern Europe, and beyond.

It was an exciting journey! Everything was possible and innovation was the key, as it still is to this day.

It takes a "warrior spirit" to navigate through life—to seek opportunities, challenge the odds, deal with the curveballs and the unforeseen. The unexpected awaits every day. The secret is to stay the course, and to not easily take "no" for an answer. There is always another angle, and a new day brings new perspectives and a clearer path forward. Because it's not what happens to you in life, it's how you deal with it.

I see myself in that picture—the young soldier who had her little army of siblings to guide—and I realize how foretelling it was. No one succeeds alone,

and my youth gave me the confidence to push boundaries, and to work in a collaborative spirit.

Today, I have the honour to be the second Canadian to serve as global president of the International Women's Forum. I am excited to steer the organization in a purposeful way and to create fresh opportunities for the advancement for future women leaders. Life is a canvas, and, with time, experiences, learnings, and failures layer to create new textures, shapes, and colours that ultimately become a unique painting—a work of art of one's life.

DEBORAH SHANNON TRUDEAU is senior VP of international business and licensing at Trudeau Corporation, a private company specializing in the development and distribution of its own kitchenware products. Trudeau is vice-chair of the board of the Royal Canadian Mint, and serves as VP of the board of the Community Foundation of Greater Montreal and on the board of governors of St. Mary's Hospital. Trudeau was elected president of the International Women's Forum in 2018.

JULIE CAFLEY

I WAS GIVING IT my all. I was three. And my grandpa was looking at me like I was the *best* singer in the world. No inhibitions. Utter confidence. No concerns about how my rendition might be perceived or interpreted. Pure love. Of course, he didn't tell me that I was tone deaf. Maybe I wasn't then? Did that unconditional love in my grandpa's eyes help make me fearless? Of course it did.

By Tibetan wisdom, humans have only two basic emotions: love and fear. And as we grow and change, we dance between the two. They coexist as contrasts, inviting a continuous choice for a lens through which to see the world. We think, speak, and act either out of love or fear. For me, this analogy is particularly relevant for women in leadership roles.

I had the privilege of a childhood that was rooted in love. This love and energy was and is my foundation. Struggles, challenges, and hardship didn't pass me by, but I had roots that made every challenge and fear seem surmountable.

Life's failure and pain taught me important lessons. I had to unlearn fear many times. The death of a parent at a young age, the divorce of my parents—and then my own divorce—speaking truth to power in the workplace, saying yes when no was much easier—there have been many times in my life when fear seemed to be an easier path forward. And, in fact, it has been in moments of fear that I have been even more propelled to love. To lead with kindness. To dare. To trust. To change. To act. To choose love over fear.

Early in my career, I asked a leader whom I respected how he knew it was time to move on and change roles. He explained that his favourite job was always the one he was in. Being in a job that he loved was central to his career success, as it is to mine.

So many people aren't happy with their jobs. Why? The answer always circles back to fear. Study after study shows the effects of fear on women's leadership paths. Many women say no to advancement, as they underestimate their abilities when applying for increasingly senior positions. Fear. An internal Hewlett Packard report indicated that women apply for roles if they meet 100 percent of the requirements, while men might apply if they hold 60 percent. Fear. We also see fear represented in the 2019 Edelman Trust Barometer—women in the general population show distrust in fifteen out of twenty-seven markets, four more markets than men.

By Tibetan wisdom, humans have only two basic emotions: love and fear. And as we grow and change, we dance between the two.

Women are redefining leadership at a time when we are craving authenticity in leaders. The public is less interested in status driven by ego, but is rather interested in strength, positive change, and—dare I say?—kindness. The Edelman Trust Barometer reveals that "my employer" is the most trusted institution, at 75 percent. How can female leaders leverage and amplify this trust in the workplace and beyond?

As a three-year-old girl, I wasn't likely singing in tune, but I was "all in." And, since then, many have told me to mouth the words, or have changed their mind about wanting me to sing a good-night lullaby. And yet I still want to sing. And women still want to lead. We want to do it differently and we want to create our own leadership norms. We want to cause a paradigm shift. And if we keep on being fearless, and we keep on singing, we will break down the ways that "things have always been done" and we will, forevermore, continue to lead, unwaveringly, with kindness. We will bring about necessary change and we will rise above fear.

———————

The executive vice president at the Public Policy Forum, JULIE CAFLEY is an accomplished leader, academic, and change-maker with expertise in higher education leadership and governance. In her previous role as chief of staff to two presidents at the University of Ottawa, she played a key role in profile-raising, fundraising, and internal communications. Cafley's PhD thesis focused on higher education leadership and governance through the lens of unfinished terms of Canadian university presidents.

CLARE BECKTON

RACING ACROSS A field to be at the front is me at age four. Growing up poor on a small farm in Saskatchewan with three brothers, I had to find my own place or be left behind. At this early age, I was displaying the sense of adventure that would lead me to places I could not have imagined.

Our farm had a lot of space, and I learned to roam our property, seeking berries and ponds to skate on, and learning about the ecosystem that supports us. Resilience was part of life, as nature always wins—weather, hail, dust storms, grasshopper infestations, drought—and I learned to persist by watching my father carry on despite the setbacks. This was a valuable early lesson, because I had many setbacks of my own on my path to success. Growing up with three brothers taught me to work with men, which helped when I later had to work in male-dominated organizations.

When I was seventeen, I announced to my parents that I was going by train to Vancouver to meet an aunt, using my earnings as a part-time telephone operator. I travelled alone—my first of many adventures far from home. Determination, hard work, openness to change, being afraid and doing it anyway, getting back up after setbacks, and an independent spirit took me from that poor family farm to law school, then to Illinois for graduate school, then on a backpack trip solo across Europe before teaching law in Nova Scotia. As the only woman in a faculty of thirty-three for my first three years, that grit and resilience were necessary to survive, and then to thrive.

There, I also learned to scuba dive, fly an airplane, and shoot a pistol—all to overcome my fears of water, flying, and guns. Nine years later, I was invited to the halls of power in Ottawa, where I worked with politicians, ministers, and deputy ministers on leading issues of the day—such as coordinating a review of federal legislation to bring it in line with the equality guarantees of the Charter. Indigenous fishing rights, foreign overfishing, new reforms to social programs, land claims, residential schools, and, ultimately, women's issues as head of Status of Women Canada were a few of the other opportunities and challenges. It was never an easy path.

In 2004, when I was in my fifties, I applied for and won a Fulbright scholarship to attend the Harvard Kennedy School and pursue a mid-career master's degree in public administration. I ended up in university at the same time as my two sons, and had an amazing experience creating a worldwide network of fellow learners. Fortunately, I could call my sons when I needed help with computer challenges.

I am constantly reminded of the importance of continuing to have dreams and goals, no matter our age.

Retired from a long career as a senior executive, and now rewired, I am pursuing my passion for advancing women's leadership. In January I was asked by an NGO to provide training for some women in Jordan. I looked at all the ominous warnings about security, and read all the safety disclaimers in the proposed contract for services. Then I decided to go anyway. During a desert tour to Petra on that trip, we made a stop at this giant sand dune. Unable to resist the challenge, I had to throw off my shoes like a child and climb to the top to see the glorious view. In this photo, I see the same determination I had when I was a child.

In all of my adventures, I am constantly reminded of the importance of continuing to have dreams and goals, no matter our age. This phase of my life is different because I am so fortunate to be able to focus entirely on my passion, and I can accept new challenges that were not possible when I had a job. I am incredibly grateful for the gifts that I have received, and for the joy of being open enough to take the many great opportunities that have and, I know, will continue to come my way.

CLARE BECKTON is an award-winning champion for the advancement of women's leadership, and the author of *Own It: Your Success, Your Future, Your Life*. She is a former professor of law, served as the head of Status of Women Canada, and is the founder of the Centre for Women in Politics and Public Leadership.

JOANNE FEDEYKO

IN THE MID 1960s, my dad and his father went into farming. I grew up on that farm, which was five hundred miles north of Edmonton. I realized much later in life that my father and grandfather were what we today call "entrepreneurs." I like to think that I learned a lot from them: independence, confidence, a willingness to try new things, and failure.

When I was fifteen, I learned how to drive a tractor called a Steiger. My dad taught me so I could help disc the field—chopping up the ground to get it ready for planting. Driving that thing was awesome and scary at the same time: when I had questions, like what to do about an oil leak, I would use the radio to call my dad, ending the conversation before I reached the end of the field, because I wasn't yet good enough to turn the Steiger around and talk at the same time.

Growing up on that farm in the 1970s and '80s, so far away from any city, I had no idea how big the world was. And I'm not sure I knew how to dream big.

But in 1999, I moved to the San Francisco Bay Area. And just like when I was learning to drive the Steiger, I was scared and excited at the same time. I had the opportunity to work for an early-stage start-up (unfortunately not Google, Apple, or Facebook), and that's where I learned what a good leader looks like and how easy it is to incorporate philanthropy into my life. I left the start-up and had the privilege of running a non-profit—an after-school running program that helps young girls build self esteem. I didn't have a clue what to do, but I dug in and applied the tenacity that I learned on the farm, the strong work ethic I learned from my dad, the business skills I learned at school, and the generosity I learned from people along the way.

In 2014 I met Asa Mathat, an accomplished photographer whom I'm now humbled to call a friend. At the time, he was working on his Big Pink Ribbon project in support of breast cancer, and he asked if he could photograph me. I wanted to say yes, but I said no. Thankfully, he asked again (and again), and eventually I found the courage to say yes. He had already photographed some of the greatest technology and world leaders of the day, so it's not surprising that I found myself once again both scared and excited. Asa encouraged me to be bold and confident. He encouraged me to be vulnerable. I had seen the images of the other men and women he photographed for the project, and everyone else seemed to be so fearless. I figured I needed to take a breath and be fearless as well. Without a doubt, Asa captured all of the emotions that I was feeling—from fear to fearless—underneath that pink sheet.

We all have pivotal moments in our lives when we need to be bold. Courageous. Fearless. Confident. When we need to ignore the voice in our head that wants to hold us back, and instead trust that taking that one step, no matter how small it is, will lead us closer to our goals and to making a difference in the world.

Being strong. Finding confidence. Relentlessly pursuing your dreams. This is not accomplished overnight, and it isn't a solo journey. Allow friends and colleagues to lift you up along the way, and don't forget to encourage people to dream big, even if it's scary.

JOANNE FEDEYKO grew up on a farm in Northern Alberta, moving to the Bay Area in 1999. After working in the consulting, start-up, and non-profit sectors, in 2016 she started Connection Silicon Valley to help connect Canadian companies with Silicon Valley tech and innovation. In 2018, she helped launch the Canadian Women's Network to support women in tech.

JILL EARTHY

THESE PICTURES SHOW me first at a time when I was transitioning between childhood into adulthood (but caught in between), and then later in my career, when I was equally goofy but leaning into my power in a different way.

Looking at the first picture, I remember feeling insecure, but also curious about my new independence, testing it with my parents, and also myself. The picture was from a trip on a small, twenty-five-foot boat with my immediate family of five. I wanted to be cool but didn't know how. I remember feeling safe and relaxed, but trapped in this small space with my family, who I felt did not understand the person I was becoming.

I love the concept of being fearless, and I continue to strive to feel this way. Each experience we have, each phase of our lives, and each of our memories shape us, and shape our perception of what it means to be fearless. When I think about the term, I am considering it from the perspective of a life that was safe and privileged. I never had to fear for my life, or wonder

where my next meal would come from. I do struggle with confidence each and every day, but I am grateful that I can explore this from a solid and secure foundation.

This second picture is from the 2018 We for She, an annual event to empower the next generation of women that I co-chair along with the amazing Lois Nahirney. Now in its sixth year, it brings together male and female business leaders with young women in grades 10 to 12 who are navigating critical years in their lives and considering the next steps in their own story.

As co-chair, I have the honour of shaping the event and speaking to the audience. The energy in the room, combined with the intelligence and optimism of the attendees, fills me with a sense of fearlessness. There is a recognition that if others can be vulnerable and share their story, then I can, too.

I was always shy, but I have learned that if I am passionate about the topic and I can feel the energy of the room, then my fear of public speaking

Each experience we have, each phase of our lives, and each of our memories shape us, and shape our perception of what it means to be fearless.

disappears. I often remind myself that we are all humans, each with our unique story and our unique fears. It is how we handle them, and engage others, that is the key.

When I see that picture of a twelve-year-old girl (especially now, as a mom to twelve- and fifteen-year-old daughters), I can't believe that I now have the opportunity, through my work and through personal connections, to embrace my fears each and every day. I am consistently placed in leadership roles to address sensitive issues, champion change, and support the next generation for gender equity. In that sense, I guess I have created my own definition of being fearless, as I have found a way to use my passion and embrace that fear. I hope to continue to support others to create their own definitions.

———————

JILL EARTHY is head of Female Funders (powered by Highline BETA), which empowers female leaders to shape the future of funding. She is on the boards of Sustainable Development Technology Canada and the Women's Enterprise Centre, and is co-chair of We for She. She was recently recognized by the CCDI as a Community Champion, by *Business in Vancouver* as an Influential Woman in Business 2019, and by WXN in 2018 among their Top 100 most powerful women in Canada.

TERESA MARQUES

BOTH OF THESE pictures were taken on my birthday—albeit with a few years in between—but they represent so much more change than just the passing of time. The first depicts a joyous me, a child delighting only in thoughts of cake and celebration. The second photo is who I am now: I still enjoy cake, of course, but now I also have an unshakable sense of loyalty and humour in tough times, and an empathy that guides everything I do.

My father was a classics professor, and my greatest influence. Growing up in Ottawa with parents in academia and teaching meant summers largely "off"—and many of them in Cape Breton, my mother's childhood home. I had so much freedom there—I would get on my brother's BMX bike every morning and head off to explore all day. Those are memories I hold dear: that sense of adventure, freedom, and curiosity you have when you're young. That excitement, of stretching yourself beyond what's safe and familiar, is thankfully still with me. More often than not, those things that give you a tight feeling in your stomach are the right thing to do.

You need to be a little bit uncomfortable, a little bit scared, or you're not pushing yourself. And you're guaranteed to have more fun along the way.

When I was fourteen, my father was diagnosed with early onset Alzheimer's, and from then to the age of twenty-two I cared for him at home with my mom. Without question, this was an extraordinarily hard, sad, sometimes lonely, and often frustrating time. But I know now that these years were integral to becoming who I am today, and I am grateful. I don't know if your values are always inside you, or if they become honed in a situation like that, but in those years I learned about responsibility, compassion, and commitment to family. I went through something very tough at a pivotal age, and my role became the calm in a storm.

Today, I still live that calm, and I lean into my quiet. I know I'm not the loudest person in the room, and that can sometimes be equated with not being ambitious, or not being confident. But it's not that at all. I take a lot of comfort in reflection, and I've learned to embrace it. It's become a part of my leadership style.

I can see now how all the pieces fit together, and how the events of my life have led me to become the leader I want to be. I know to trust my own instincts, to embrace my strengths, and to use them to build my team. To some extent, that trust has come from experience, but it also has to do with simply being more comfortable in my own skin. And I still laugh—a lot.

———————

TERESA MARQUES is an important voice in Canada as president and CEO at the Rideau Hall Foundation, where she works to support the foundation's vision of a better Canada, with a focus on equity of learning opportunities, culture of innovation, leadership development, and promotion of giving and volunteerism.

ULRIKE BAHR-GEDALIA

THIS WAS A turning point for me. At just eight years old, I was discovering the person I wanted to become. I wanted to take risks, to be vocal, courageous, a disrupter and a change-maker.

Looking back at this photo of myself, sitting on this majestic creature, enjoying a summer vacation with my family on Amrum, an island in Germany, I realize something: this moment in my life represents the horsepower I needed to follow my passions, challenge the status quo, and embrace every challenge as an opportunity. While I was still being led with the help of a leash, I learned early on that you have to take risks, stand up, stand out, and be uncomfortable at times to see where it can take you. I also learned that, as you move from being led to becoming a leader, you always have to remain open to listening and learning from others—and I've been fortunate to have had numerous roles models in my life I could look up to.

This was also the year I joined an all-boys soccer team, which I stayed in for six straight years. At the time, this was completely unheard of—especially in my small town. I could have waited to join a female league at sixteen, but that would have meant waiting eight long years to fulfill my dream! I played well, I loved to play, and, most importantly, I made an impact. I redefined the perception that girls could not play on the boys' team, and became a leader on the field, with the support and recognition of my coach, team, parents, and even the fans. This fearless girl became a role model for other girls

who were waiting for their chance to shine on the soccer field. At only eight years old, I proved that what others thought was impossible was actually far from it. Taking no for an answer is not something I agree with—I believe in challenging false perceptions and driving positive disruption.

For me, that year—the year I rode the horse and joined my soccer team—set my path in motion. These two experiences literally unleashed my potential and the ball was now in my court. It shaped my perspective on leadership.

Today, I stand here as the president and CEO of Nova Scotia's ICT and digital technologies sector industry association—without a degree in computer science or expert coding knowledge—challenging false perceptions. Decades later, with degrees in political science and in film, literature, and linguistics, I am a leader in tech with twenty years in the industry. Much like it was on the soccer field, I am often one of very few women in the boardroom, and one of few in my sector.

I learned early on that you have to take risks, stand up, stand out, and be uncomfortable at times to see where it can take you.

The moment this second photo was taken was one of peace, fulfillment, accomplishment, and happiness. I was reminded of the day I sat on that horse, except, instead of looking forward at who I wanted to become, I was able to reflect on who I am. My dreams as an eight-year-old on the horse and on the soccer field allowed me to become the person I am today, taking the stage, sharing my knowledge, and being a voice for those who might not have one. I've travelled the world; taken a gap year in California; studied in Texas; lived and worked in Israel, the UK, and the Netherlands; learned six languages; moved from film and philology to information technology; and— something that is most precious to me—raised a son and daughter together with my wonderful husband.

The horsepower I realized it would take to get me started has carried me through life so far, and my journey has only just begun.

With a career spanning five geographic regions, ULRIKE BAHR-GEDALIA is a multilingual, award-winning innovator, entrepreneur, and TEDX speaker with over twenty years of experience in the private, public, non-profit, and academic sectors. Originally from Germany, Bahr-Gedalia immigrated from Israel to Canada in 2002, where she lives with her spouse, son, and daughter. Ulrike is currently president and CEO of Digital Nova Scotia.

SERVE

"REAL CHANGE,
ENDURING CHANGE,
HAPPENS ONE
STEP AT A TIME."

Ruth Bader Ginsburg

Where Sacrifice and Leadership Meet

ANY TIME I have moved into a new home, the first order of operations is to put up a new Canadian flag. Each house feels like a home as soon as that maple leaf is flapping in the wind and standing on guard.

As a proud Canadian, when I'm speaking on a global stage, I love to weave in the unique Canadian perspective. I had the chance to do so when I spoke at the Milken Conference in 2018 in Los Angeles. It was a highlight for me to offer the Canadian perspective on women, diversity, and inclusion, and also to talk about my national research on women entrepreneurs. The best example I had to show of the Canadian commitment to inclusion was in regard to our national anthem. By changing a few words, the English-language version of the anthem became gender neutral. Although only a small difference, it was a powerful signal of our support for inclusion. With a change of the second line of the anthem from "in all thy sons command" to "in all of us command," this version now reflects all Canadians. Most people at the conference were unaware of the change, and were moved by Canada's decision to be fully inclusive in our national anthem.

While I have never served in the military, I have deep admiration for those who do. Similarly, I admire those who choose public service as a career.

Canadian women have played an important role in the military since they first answered the call to service in 1885 during the North-West Rebellion, when twelve women served in military hospitals. The Canadian Armed Forces was one of the first to open all military occupations to women, and today is focused on increasing the representation of women across all trades and ranks. The goal is that, by 2026, one in four CAF members will be women.

The Canadian women who serve and our American sisters highlighted here are willing to make the ultimate sacrifice. Their commitment is strong and unwavering and our countries and the world are better because of their decision to serve. These are moving stories of women who have forged new pathways in environments that have not always been inclusive or inviting places for women to lead. And yet, through hard work, commitment, and determination, they have found a way to do exactly that.

JANICE

CHRIS WHITECROSS

I WOULDN'T SAY WE came from a poor family, because we had every thing we needed, and we had parents who cared for us—but we certainly didn't have any extras. The unusual dress in the photo on the next page was made by my mother, who was an accomplished seamstress—more for practicability reasons than anything else—and I was proud of it. I was also very unconscious of my looks; they just didn't matter. Truth is, back then I was just happy to be alive and getting my photo taken! I saw the world through my very limited and very little (I was always the smallest in the class) lens, and my world was ok.

I was tremendously naive and shy growing up. I didn't understand innuendo, and that made me seem a bit odd to my classmates. But that didn't matter, because I was also incredibly positive—life was good and things could only get better! Was I fearless? Not really. I hated confrontation and craved being liked, and it was important to me that I did the right thing. I wasn't anyone special. Family was my anchor.

There are a few similarities between that young girl and who I am now. I am still less preoccupied with my physical appearance than I am with my actual presence. There is more maturity and less ultraism in my eyes. I have seen some pretty harsh things in my military career—things my younger self wouldn't have been able to process if she had seen it, things that would have caused her to turn inward. But I have also seen some tremendously

Nothing comes from us alone— especially not success—teamwork, professionalism, hard work: these are the hallmarks of what defines us, and my younger self knew this.

inspiring things, too. And those moments would have reconfirmed the way my younger self saw the world.

I started my military career as a quiet individual who joined to serve her country. I was positive by nature, and this helped me get through training. It also helped me to fit in. I worked hard in everything I did—school, sports, engineering—so doing the same in my career was second nature. I had no concept of inequality, because everything in my life up to that point was equal, as I understood it. I think this helped me, because I didn't look for inequality in my work or personal life. I just worked hard, and got out of my career what I put into it.

Growing up in uniform, I never thought I was anything special—just like when I was young. Promotions surprised me, positive comments mystified me—I was no different from anyone else. I truly believe that this humility has been the greatest gift my younger self ever gave me. Nothing comes from us alone—especially not success—teamwork, professionalism, hard work: these are the hallmarks of what defines us, and my younger self knew this.

My younger self, though, would have had difficulties standing up for herself, especially in the presence of authority. She would have been too timid to speak out to express her discomfort or to share her concerns. The older I get and the more responsibility I have, the more I realize how imperative this is. Standing up for myself is a legacy I hope to give my own children—it took me a while to embrace who I was and to know that I belong, and, more importantly, that I have something to say and something to offer.

Today, I am blessed with the best combination—of both of me.

———————

Commandant of the Rome NATO Defense College, LIEUTENANT GENERAL CHRIS WHITECROSS has a BEng, MDS, and is a graduate of the Advanced Military Studies and Command and Staff Courses. A Commander of the Order of Military Merit, she was named one of Canada's Top 100 Most Powerful Women of 2011 and 2016; and was the 2018 recipient of the CDAI Vimy Award.

SOLANGE TUYISHIME

THIS CHILDHOOD PHOTO is a representation of the dreams I have for every girl in this world: love, safety, and belonging. This is truly the one time I can remember being genuinely happy and fearless, with dreams of being on a world stage—inspiring and engaging people globally.

As a young girl I had everything a child could need and want. A loving family, a safe environment, and a great education, surrounded by friends and family who brought much joy to my life. I belonged.

For the rest of my life, I would struggle with that word: belonging. Where do I belong, and what is my happiness?

At eleven years old, I survived a war genocide, and witnessed family members suffer, lose their lives, and lose hope for all the great things this world has to offer. In that moment of trauma, I would unconsciously be inked with a new, limiting belief that there was no such thing as true happiness.

In a matter of days, I went from living in a beautiful home to sharing one tent with my entire family. I watched as my family lost everything and struggled to make ends meet. I could see and feel the fear in all of us for our survival, safety, and well-being.

I watched mothers cry for the survival of their children, grown men feel hopeless, children become orphans, and millions of people facing despair, disease, violence, and exploitation. Living through those moments came with the greatest lesson of my life: pain knows no colours, ethnicity, or nationality; hate has no place in our society. In that moment, as a child, I would commit my life to making this world a better place.

Two years from then, I would travel in four countries as a refugee, each time having to teach myself how to survive and fit in. In those times, I was inked with my second limiting belief: that there is no such thing as true belonging, because the world is a cruel place that can take away everything you have and love at any given moment. So I silently loved people and places, without ever saying it out loud or showing it too much—fearing that it might one day be taken away from me.

To move forward, I've had to redefine what happiness means for me. Today, I trust that happiness is in the moments we live, in the love we give and obtain, in the kindness we experience from those who are near and dear, and from those who are strangers. Happiness is the pure moments of gratitude we give ourselves the right to feel. Happiness is the freedom within our hearts.

Today, I find my belonging in the service of that eleven-year-old girl's promise. I belong in uniting heart-centred and inclusive leaders, so that they can continue to be inspired to make the decisions that will make this world better. I belong in the service of women who are ready and more than qualified to take on leadership roles in our society, and I belong in the service of the millions of girls around the world who are patiently waiting for us to give them a glimpse of hope and a path toward great health, education, and equality.

So while the stage I am building for the heart-centred leaders of this world is not yet as big as the ones I had in my dreams at eleven years old... this recent photo is proof of inspiration and hope for every girl, that we become phenomenal women. And I am one step in the right direction.

SOLANGE TUYISHIME is an international speaker, social entrepreneur, and philanthropist. She is president and CEO of Elevate International, co-founder of Naylah's Legacy, and a UNICEF Canada Ambassador. In her leadership role, Tuyishime has dedicated her life to elevating women and girls through the advancement of leadership, economic growth, and community building. As a UNICEF Canada Ambassador, she works to help save the lives of mothers and children living in unfortunate circumstances.

LORRAINE BEN

WE FLED BELFAST with few belongings to start a new life away from the bombings and violence that surrounded us. That young girl in the black and white photograph snacking on carnival popcorn was fierce and feisty. She saw opportunity in this new land, but was surrounded by uncertainty as her parents were just barely able to make ends meet.

Several decades later, after cutting her teeth in the male-dominated worlds of telecommunications and defence sales, that young girl has become a grown lady—standing in full colour in front of the impressive fifth-generation stealth fighter jet, the F-35. She is a leader, a mentor, and a key decision maker for the Canadian arm of Lockheed Martin, considered one of the world's largest and top-ranking defence companies.

I chose the photos you see in this story because they depict my life in worlds apart and represent the humble beginnings that always remain a constant source of grounding in my life. As a child, I had a big imagination and lofty dreams—but never did I dream that I'd find myself at the helm of a corporate office.

I can truly say that the person I am today is still, at the very core, that young girl born of hardship, facing adversity and challenges as a new immigrant with a unique accent, but seeing opportunity to be someone who could make a difference.

During the terrorist attacks of 9/11, I was living in Owego, New York, working for a division of Lockheed Martin that supported the US Postal

Service and travelling to Washington on a regular basis. The climate of my daily life changed in an instant, as it did for millions of Americans. Having just had my son and witnessing firsthand the devastation and toll of the terrorist attacks, I struggled to better understand how I could contribute. After returning home to Canada in 2003 with my husband Rob and our two-year-old son Nicolas, I was determined to find a way to support our troops.

In 2007 I did exactly that—I led a team to win the largest global defence contract in telecommunications. Working alongside military personnel inspired

me to want to do more for our men and women in uniform. It became a natural fit for me. Canada's soldiers, sailors, and airmen and women are truly
our natural resources, and it's their dedication to our defence and security
that keeps me driving forward to provide the most capable products and
solutions to bring them home safely.

Throughout my life I have had a thirst for learning and for trying something new. These traits guided me to always strive for improvement. I wanted
to do great things in my career, but I was shy in a sea of accomplished men. I
had to force myself out of my comfort zone on so many occasions by stepping
up to the table, leaning in, and occasionally taking the stage.

Being knowledgeable in your craft—your specialty—gives you the confidence to be a leader, and to take smart risks.

Being knowledgeable in your craft—your specialty—gives you the confidence to be a leader, and to take smart risks.

Coming full circle, in 2015 I had the opportunity to take a leadership role at Lockheed Martin Canada and was recently appointed the company's national chief executive. We are at a critical juncture in defence procurement in Canada, and our company has a significant responsibility to deliver on major contracts to the Royal Canadian Navy, the Canadian Army, and the Royal Canadian Air Force. The selection of Canada's future fighter jet will impact our nation for generations to come, and I find myself leading through difficult conversations while providing strategic focus and vision. It's a daunting task—but one I know I've prepared for all my life, and one that I wouldn't be able to accomplish without the support of the amazing leaders, mentors, and friends who have guided me on this journey.

LORRAINE BEN is an Irish immigrant who grew up in Sault Ste. Marie, graduated from Laurentian University, and has held numerous business development and sales positions throughout her career, leading to her current role as chief executive of Lockheed Martin Canada. She married her best friend from high school, Rob Ben, with whom she shares a son, Nicolas.

PAULINA CAMERON

TO BE COURAGEOUS in the face of fear feels like a must to me. We live in a world of urgent needs, all of which require us to choose courage over comfort, to answer the call to make an impact, and to use our voice for change. It's a time of great opportunity, and a time when we must show up as our fearless selves to lead and to catalyze.

The photo on the facing page of my adult self embodies such a time for me—here I am, a few months into my new role leading an organization whose purpose I am so deeply passionate about, with my two-week-old baby girl in my arms. By showing up for both roles—with great support, I must add—I hope to offer an additional narrative of working parenthood, one where it's an "and" as opposed to an "either or."

Being a leader and being a mother present daily, sometimes hourly, opportunities to step into fearlessness in order to do what needs to be done. In both roles there are many moments where I am in the unknown, relying on my values, instinct, and prayer to carry me through. As someone who likes to know the answers, this is an uncomfortable space for me. I can muster the courage when I remember that it truly is a muscle, one that, when exercised, becomes stronger. When I remind myself that acts of fearlessness don't

often feel that way in the moment, but only when we look back on them. And when I reach out for wisdom and support from the women in my life.

There are many things I love about the picture of my young self—how it calls to mind the love and devotion of my parents, who sacrificed greatly immigrating us to Canada, and for how it captures the essence of strength and joy so well. Here I am, about seven years old, on the top of a literal mountain in beautiful Whistler, British Columbia. I love the pride I can see in my face—if I close my eyes I can feel it, that moment when you get to the top of the mountain you were hiking and you turn around and, for the first time, you can see the view you worked hard to reach. It's a sense of deep satisfaction, pride, sweat, and awe. It's the moment where we recognize our courage, our fearlessness. (I'd be lying if I didn't admit that I also love how I'm rocking my outfit—entirely mismatched, likely hand-me-downs, with not a care in the world about it. I wish I could channel that attitude more sometimes. I hear it comes with age, and I'm so here for it.)

When I think of my younger self, particularly in the pre-teen years—which, let's face it, are typically like a rollercoaster for girls—I remember embodying relentless optimism, the kind of lightness that a glass-half-full mentality holds. I am grateful for that mindset, as, to this day, it has served me well in continuously seeking and pursuing opportunities for impact and visions greater than myself.

PAULINA CAMERON spends her days thinking about equity, connections, and impact. As the CEO of the Forum for Women Entrepreneurs, she elevates women entrepreneurs, and as the bestselling author of *Canada 150 Women*, she curates stories of inspirational women. She serves her community as a board director for the YWCA Greater Vancouver, the Immigrant Employment Council of BC and the Government of BC's Small Business Roundtable. Cameron is married, and mother to two children.

JEAN TERON

LOOKING AT MY 1956 Carleton University grad photo, I remember a happy girl, but one who lacked any confidence. With a new husband who was starting two businesses, I became the company bookkeeper and sold Scandinavian furniture in our shop. As four children came along, I started volunteering in the community for the Cancer Society, the Salvation Army, Red Feather (now United Appeal), and the Kidney Foundation.

Getting involved with the Carleton Alumni Association with some fundraising, I was stunned one day when the then-chair of the Associates of Carleton, a 1970s support group of citizens, asked me to become its next chair (I would be the first woman to take the role). To have to speak in public was a terrifying, but I said yes. A few years later an invitation came to join the Carleton board of governors—a role I could never have dreamed of a few decades earlier. In 1983, to my astonishment, I later became the first woman board chair, a role I held until 1986. I was also serving on the boards of the Kidney Foundation and the Trillium Foundation.

Another huge interest in my life has been Ashbury College. It was challenging but rewarding to chair a major fundraising campaign there, and later to co-chair another one. That involvement led to becoming the board chair at Ashbury, where again I was the first woman to hold the role. I never put my own name up, and I must give that credit to men. Every time I was asked to take on a new role, the request came from a man. I hear so much about women lacking the self-confidence to seek the next promotion, about underrating themselves. And that was me. I could never have agreed to take on the roles I did if others didn't have more confidence in me than I had in myself.

Fundraising has been a part of my life in several organizations—the Ottawa Hospital Foundation, Canada's National Arts Centre, the Ottawa Chamber Music Society. Many people shy away from fundraising, saying, "I could never ask anyone for money," but I have never found it difficult when you truly believe in the cause. In fact, asking for a donation is an opportunity to boast about the organization and its goals.

To this day I feel so fortunate to be able to stay in touch with Carleton and Ashbury, allowing me to witness the commitment of the next generation in confronting the challenges and opportunities of climate change. Ottawa is such a great place to live. It's a vibrant, large city now, but it's also small in many good ways—it's so friendly and responsive to one's efforts.

The ultimate surprise came a few years ago, when I was awarded an honourary degree from Carleton. It was an unbelievable approval of my career, and I often found myself singing the tune from *The Sound of Music* that says "somewhere in my youth or childhood, I must have done something good."

JEAN TERON (née Woodwark) was born in Ottawa, Ontario, in 1936. She graduated from Carleton University in 1956, and worked for her husband, Bill Teron, until volunteering in the community became a bigger role. She still supports and volunteers with several organizations, such as Carleton University, the Ottawa Hospital Foundation, Ashbury College, and the Ottawa Chamber Music Society. Teron has four children and seven grandchildren.

JULIA DEANS

'D LIKE TO think I was born fearless, but my mother and grandmother made it inevitable by inspiring me to always embrace new opportunities to learn, be challenged, and help others when needed.

Both were single mothers with successful careers focused on public service. As a senior civil servant, my grandmother helped launch the Stratford Festival and worked to settle Dutch immigrants in Ontario, while my mother's leadership, communication, and fundraising prowess has boosted the impact of non-profit organizations in Canada and around the world. They were always curious, compassionate, ambitious, and intrepid, and they expected no less from me.

At two years old, I couldn't have known what a stimulating life and career I would have. But I look at the photo on the next page and see that my eyes are wide open, trusting, and looking straight ahead, with a hint of the spirit that has kept me moving forward through sometimes uncertain and difficult times.

My Australian father sailed to a new life in Canada as a Rotary Fellow in the late 1950s. Inspired by him and by my mother, I love immersing myself in new places and cultures and the expanded perspective and empathy this brings. When my equally intrepid husband was offered a role in Hong Kong, we jumped on it. I left a traditional legal career in Toronto to do wildly varied legal and business development work throughout Asia. Living through Hong Kong's handover to China was fascinating, especially seeing firsthand the fierce determination to remain independent that so characterizes Hong Kong people.

Moving to Singapore, I decided to test my entrepreneurial skills and opened the South East Asian operations of a UK-based legal recruitment firm. I loved the challenge of creating a successful new venture in a country where I knew no one, and it was satisfying to help build many law firms and legal careers throughout Asia.

Returning to Canada, I took several years to get my children acclimatized and threw myself into volunteer work. I learned how to motivate people when you aren't paying them. This proved helpful when I returned to paid work as CEO of CivicAction and had to develop innovative cross-sectoral initiatives and keep the organization moving forward following the untimely death of its extraordinary founding chair, David Pecaut.

David helped me hone my convening and leadership skills, which I now use to help others succeed in the most impactful ways I can find. From helping young people realize their entrepreneurial dreams to charting ways to help immigrants prosper to creating a plan to improve children's literacy, I look for opportunities to use all of my education, experiences, and skills to create more opportunities for others.

I look at this photo and see that my eyes are wide open, trusting, and looking straight ahead, with a hint of the spirit that has kept me moving forward through sometimes uncertain and difficult times.

I am now a woman with a stimulating life and career. As the photo at the start of this story shows, my eyes are still wide open, trusting, and looking straight ahead, now confident in the spirit and determination that serve me so well in uncertain times.

With degrees from Queen's, Columbia, and Osgoode Hall Law School, JULIA DEANS practiced law with Torys in Toronto and Hong Kong and built QD Legal in Singapore before becoming a non-profit CEO with CivicAction, Futurpreneur Canada, and the Canadian Children's Literacy Foundation. She is also a director of many non-profit and business organizations.

JOSÉE KURTZ

AS LONG AS I can remember, I have wanted to wear a uniform. My first recollection of noticing a uniform was when I was running errands with my mom, and I saw the driver of city bus we were riding. I was no more than four years old, but I can still clearly see the grey outfit and the hat. A few years later, our neighbours' son enrolled in the Canadian Armed Forces, and I was smitten with his stories every time he came home to visit. That's when I decided that I would join the military as well.

I wore my first uniform when I became a sea cadet. At the local corps, I experienced structure and discipline, acquired seamanship and leadership skills, and made lifelong friends. I spent hours preparing my uniform and polishing my boots, and I could not wait for the weekly meeting, during which I would involve myself in as many activities as possible—from the drill team to band—and I always sought out additional duties and greater responsibilities. Those were formative years for me, and a door to an environment from which, until then, women had been largely excluded.

I did not, however, see that as an obstacle. I took it as a challenge.

I was nineteen years old when I joined the Royal Canadian Navy by happenstance. When I arrived at the recruiting centre I did not have a preference for any particular occupation (as you recall, I just really wanted to wear the uniform). Seeing that I had been a sea cadet and that the Navy was, at the time, opening service at sea to women, the recruiters suggested I become a naval officer. And so I signed my initial terms of service.

That was thirty-one years ago, and I my career has been fulfilling. I have served Canada at sea on both the Atlantic and Pacific coasts and I have been deployed on missions abroad. I have had the privilege of working with wonderful people, in ships and ashore. I am also honoured to have been appointed to positions of significant responsibility, including as commanding officer of a frigate, HMS *Halifax*, in 2010, and in 2019 as commander of Standing NATO Maritime Group 2, leading an international staff and naval task group in the Mediterranean and Black Sea region for a six-month period.

These two pictures show me in uniform, then and now. If the uniform is the connection between my past and present, there is more to this than fancy buttons and shiny shoes. Dress and deportment is at the core of military ethos, and I always wear my uniform with great pride. It reflects the tenets of my personality: duty, loyalty, and tenacity—from humble beginnings riding the bus with my mother to representing Canada abroad.

JOSÉE KURTZ has thirty-one years of service as an officer in the Royal Canadian Navy. One of the first women to serve at sea, she went on to command a frigate and has reached the rank of commodore. She is currently the commander of Standing NATO Maritime Group 2, leading an international staff and naval task group operating in the Mediterranean and Black Sea region.

DEBORAH ROSATI

I **ALWAYS WANTED TO** be a businessman like my father. He was a self-made man, entrepreneurial and a well-respected leader in the community. My father was fearless in taking on bold projects in the arts and culture. His creative passion and ideas led others to follow him.

I stand here today proud to be my father's daughter. He inspires me every day to be persistent, passionate, and purposeful on my own bold projects, to never give up and to believe in myself. Thank you, Dad!

Throughout the years, I have found myself being one of few, if not the only, women around the boardroom table. As a corporate director, I bring entrepreneurial, financial, and governance expertise in the technology, retail, consumer, and cannabis sectors. I am often asked by women how I got on a corporate board, so I decided it was time to launch Women Get On Board, a member-based company. My passion is to inspire more women to lead and serve. I have learned many lessons in the twenty years since I joined my first corporate board, and I would like to share them here.

First, be fearless—use your confidence to embrace change. Be independent-minded and stand up for what you believe. Have the courage to do the right thing and be ethical in your decisions. Be brave, be decisive, and be determined. Be your authentic self—for me, I have been inspired by *The Four Agreements*, by Don Miguel Ruiz: "Be impeccable with your word. Don't take anything personally. Don't make assumptions. Always do your best."

Plan your journey and set goals. What is your strongest desire, longing, aim, or ambition? Think outside your comfort zone. Plan your path to success: where do you want to be in five, ten, or even twenty years? Tell your inner circle about your journey, goals, and plans for your future.

Be curious—explore new opportunities and solve problems. Don't be afraid to ask questions; seek to understand. Look for ways to reinvent yourself. Change is good; change is inevitable—so make change part of your life.

Get involved in your community. Seek out non-profit board opportunities and volunteer for a cause you are passionate about. You will meet people outside of your current business circle that you can help you make a difference. And always be learning, because knowledge is power! As professionals, we have to invest in our professional development and go beyond our continuing education requirements. To master a particular skill, you must invest ten thousand hours.

Be curious—explore new opportunities and solve problems. Don't be afraid to ask questions; seek to understand. Look for ways to reinvent yourself.

Speak up, stand out, and be visible. Post your insights in blogs; share in presentations or articles and on social media platforms. Comment on topics in which you have expertise. Take on leadership roles. Embrace social media, and be active, thoughtful, and relevant in your posts. Take advantage of the opportunity to build your personal brand, enhance your profile, and share your point of view and expertise. And network, network, network! Attend events that matter to you, to meet new people. Invite someone new out to lunch or coffee, and ask for introductions.

Finally, seek out mentors and sponsors. Look for a mentor outside of your organization, someone who inspires you. Seek out a sponsor—someone who will make introductions and connect you. And become a mentor to others. You will learn a lot from them!

———————

DEBORAH ROSATI is the corporate director, founder, and CEO of Women Get On Board Inc. She is an accomplished corporate director, entrepreneur, Fellow Chartered Professional Accountant (FCPA), and certified Corporate Director (ICD.D) with more than thirty years of experience in technology, consumer, retail, cannabis, private equity, and venture capital.

DREAM

"I KNOW FOR SURE
THAT WHAT WE
DWELL ON IS WHO
WE BECOME."

———

Oprah Winfrey

Infinite Possibility, Infinite Blue Sky

MANY THOUSANDS OF years ago, around 4000 B.C.E., the Egyptians became the first society to create a dream dictionary, and their ancient interpretations were used to discover clues that might help them predict the future. Today, we seek similar insight from our dreams, looking at their meaning and symbolism to tell us something about ourselves, and perhaps how we might steer our own destinies. I think Eleanor Roosevelt was right when she said, "The future belongs to those who believe in the beauty of their dreams."

The average person has almost fifteen hundred dreams a year—about four dreams per night. Most of us will spend about a quarter of a century asleep and, within that time, we are dreaming for about six years or more. If so much of our time is spent having dreams, shouldn't we make our daydreams just as big, bold, and beautiful?

When we contemplate our future by imagining the possibilities, we must never put a ceiling where there should be only blue sky. Each of us has the power to make incredible things happen. What we think about, we create. Indeed, what we imagine for ourselves is what we become.

Countless stories in this book are about women who've tapped into their own potential and are working to bring about what they wanted for themselves and for the world. They have sustained a clear vision, and their dreams have guided them into powerful and positive action. The stories of these women reflect the simple truth that a dream always precedes the reality. The women in this final chapter are part of a select crowd of dreamers. They believe in the beauty of their dreams, and have used that unwavering faith to make the impossible happen.

JANICE

NATALIE RENS

T'S 1991 IN the picture on the next page, and I am eighteen months old. I had set my sights on the engine box in our backyard, and decided I wanted to be on top of it. It made no difference that the box was as tall as me. I climbed up all on my own and, according to my mother, stood there like I owned the place.

In the years to follow, though, the last thing I felt was fearless. My family moved countries twice before I turned eight, after which I could never quite figure out how to fit in. Socially, I came to accept an identity of being "different," choosing skateboarding, colourful hair, and good grades in place of popularity. While I battled to navigate school, at home I could lean on two stellar role models. My mother, the epitome of a strong South African woman, showed me the beauty of grace in the face of adversity. Meanwhile, constant competition with my brother Justin taught me that being a girl or being younger did not entitle me to any special allowances. I was expected to step up or lose; a valuable life lesson to this day.

I continued with my early stubborn tendencies and launched myself at any challenge that offered the taste of impossibility. At ten, I fixed my sights on becoming a scientist and, envisioning a future developing cures, set the goal of winning a Nobel Prize. I impatiently finished school at age sixteen

(I had no lunch breaks for a year!) and went on to study in a further four countries, eventually earning my PhD in neuroscience. But by that point I had become disenchanted with academia, and the grand dreams I had held as a child felt buried beyond reach. I faced the decision of either accepting that this was adulthood or admitting to myself, and everyone around me, that the course I had been pursuing for over a decade was not, in fact, the right one. I was afraid.

Confronting the uncomfortable truth, I started exploring everything from international relations to professional dance in my efforts to rediscover a sense of purpose. Years passed and, finally, I started to notice little cues

My mother, the epitome of a strong South African woman, showed me the beauty of grace in the face of adversity.

that indicated I had unearthed a cause I cared intensely for. I found myself carrying a card around with me that listed facts about Mars. I tuned into space launches at work. I cried so much watching National Geographic's *Mars* series on a plane that I embarrassed the passenger seated next to me. None of this made sense to me until SpaceX successfully launched the Falcon Heavy rocket and, seeing Starman in space, I understood my impossible dream: to help humans in our journey to life in space.

In the photo at the start of this story it is 2018 and I am twenty-eight years old. It is the week that I go out on my own, registering what will become my company, Astreia. The mission is to enable sustainable human life in space. I have very little idea how to achieve that yet, but it makes no difference. Today, I do feel fearless. I count myself truly fortunate to work on a challenge for which I care so deeply that fear has become irrelevant. The worst I could do is fail, and failure is nothing but a momentary stall when you have absolute conviction in your destination.

———————

DR. NATALIE RENS is the founder of Astreia. Prior to this, Rens was the artificial intelligence specialist for the Office of the Queensland Chief Entrepreneur and co-founder of Queensland AI. Rens holds a bachelor in biomedical science (honours), a master's in cellular and molecular neuroscience, and a PhD in neuroscience.

DEBORAH MCDONALD

THIS IS WHAT joy looks like when you're eleven.

It's a full-throated roar of glee and an unwavering gaze that embraces the instant. It's fearless.

In 1976 on a balmy night in Ottawa, I celebrate Canada Day and the personal triumph of being allowed to wield a lit sparkler. It's a fire stick that sears through the darkness and leaves magical, ethereal patterns as I wave. Sparks shoot from the core but evaporate before they hit the ground. This phenomenon both delights and fascinates me. I've melted crayons on the sidewalk before and flattened pennies on the railway tracks that run behind my school. Slipping through a hole in the fence at recess to place a penny on the track leads to an enormous sense of accomplishment as I retrieve my transformed, shiny and ever so flat treasure. In time I accumulate quite a collection. And in time again, I lose track of it. Then later, I lose it for good. But on this night, it's safe in my room and, outside on the patio, the fiery sparkler captivates, as it represents not a physical transformation linked to the crayons and pennies but rather the ephemeral evidence of permanent change.

Although my parents always encourage my sisters and me to challenge our limits, up until this moment, handling anything to do with fire has been strictly off limits. And I'm generally fine with this restriction because lighting fires without purpose holds no fascination for me. But demonstrating that

I can spray lighter fluid all over the hibachi coals and then light the match without burning my fingers and then drop it to create a fiery poof without singeing my eyebrows off, all of that, just like my dad can, well, that's a matter quite entirely different. So too is my mother's ability to assemble the perfect ratio of logs to kindling and to scratch the match in just the right way to allow its momentum to ignite the fireplace without setting her sleeve on fire. We don't have the long matches so her sleeves are perpetually at risk. Now these are the firestarter opportunities I want in on. And apparently tonight, as evidenced by my lit sparkler, my parents have decided that it's time and in this moment, as the sparkler punctuates the darkness, I realize that I hold the future.

So this is what joy looks like when you're eleven.

It's fearless because it's untempered. But as an adult nuance and context must always be considered and emotions must sometimes be constrained. And I'm generally fine with these restrictions because measured matters: disciplined and informed daily steps combined with a laser focus on goals is a potent recipe for being phenomenal regardless of the endeavour. And

It's a full-throated roar of glee and an unwavering gaze that embraces the instant. It's fearless.

proceeding even in the presence of incomplete information or unknown outcomes, this grit is an adult form of fearless. But it's also always eyes fixed on the horizon, and never, albeit so briefly, a nose in the roses. There's no untempered joy baked into this formula. One day I understand this and then next I tweak the formula: I'd never be eleven again but for this to work, I didn't need to be.

As I write this I sit on my own patio in California. My gas barbeque doesn't require a match to light it and neither does my gas fireplace. Now I've accomplished many things and becoming a filmmaker is one of them.

This second picture is snapped four decades after the night of the sparkler. Here I arrive at a film festival party after my film screens to a capacity crowd and receives a standing ovation. As an artist, it doesn't get much better than that.

And so this is what joy looks like when you decide to tweak the formula so you can celebrate moments with life turned up to eleven. Look familiar? It's a full-throated roar of glee and an unwavering gaze that embraces the instant.

And that's not only fearless, it's absolutely phenomenal.

DEBORAH J. MCDONALD doesn't only embrace juxtaposition, she embodies it. She's a CPA, CA (Ernst & Young), an award-winning filmmaker (BFA University of Art SF), and part of the spatial computing new wave. She also holds a BA from the University of Toronto (political science) and is a producer (ASG) for Google Developer Studios.

STACEY BAFI-YEBOA

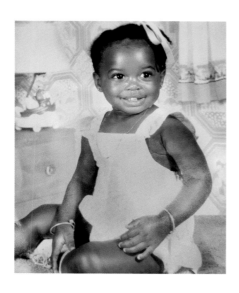

She's a ray of sunshine and is rarely seen without a smile.
A fashionista from the start,
Mama taught her to look her very best, but also taught her to be tough and never give up.
She has a sparkle in her eye, a vision in her soul,
A girly girl at heart, with a ferocious inner spirit.
If it were possible to fly, you know she'd be the first to try.

She's quiet, yet loud.
An introvert, but extrovert.
She's passionate, patient, and creative,
Yet one of the strongest competitors you'll ever face.
She lives for a challenge and is driven by defeat.
Her ride has not been easy, but she's chosen to glide through it effortlessly.

She's grateful for all her experiences and motivated to build upon them.
She sees opportunity in possibilities,
Her mission is to soar.
She's ready to pave the way and motivate others with her journey.

When I think of fearlessness, I am reminded of her, the little girl.
Inspired to dream and determined to achieve.
Deep within her soul is a drive to do the unimaginable.
Her dreams are limitless.
Then and now, little has changed!

STACEY MARTIN BAFI-YEBOA is a fashion designer and entrepreneur who started her career as a performing artist, having danced on Broadway and in films, television commercials, and movies. The Stacey Martin collection (formally KANIA) is designed with natural and sustainable fabrics for pieces that inspire the wearer to be both comfortable and fashionable.

SUSAN ST AMAND

THE PHOTO ON the next page is of me celebrating my first award for achievement, with my mother. My mother encouraged me to work hard, to love learning, and to dream big. Every year our town would celebrate the accomplishments of three young people who were active in our community and who were good students.

This one here is more recent, taken after I was unanimously elected by my peers as chair of the Ottawa International Airport Authority. I needed some new photos to use for social media when promoting YOW airport.

In both photos, I was celebrating an accomplishment and leading by example. I had worked hard, stayed true to my values, overcome some difficult obstacles, and achieved success. I felt proud, encouraged, and confident. I was looking forward to a bright future.

Recognizing and celebrating an accomplishment with family, friends, and your community is an important part of leadership. To encourage and support others, to be an example for future leaders.

I grew up in a small town "at the end of a road," as my sister would say. I was the youngest of four and in some ways we were a non-traditional family. In high school, I was told I could not take shop because it was for boys, and home economics was for girls. I was told if I continued through my chosen course of math, my future would be restricted. I was told my career choices were nurse, secretary, or teacher.

When I was a child, my mother would say, "You can do anything you want to do." I wasn't sure how, or what she meant, but I had faith that if I worked

Recognizing and celebrating an accomplishment with family, friends, and your community is an important part of leadership.

hard, kept focused, and embraced change, I would keep moving forward and find out what life had in store for me.

I am a very positive person, always looking for the silver lining and encouraged by the opportunities that change can bring. As a good friend and mentor of mine says, "There are two sides to every coin—so what is on the other side of that coin?"

I was the first woman chair of YOW, and I am proud of my accomplishments. I run my own business, because I can. I don't listen to people who say "it can't be done," and I look forward to the opportunities that change can bring. As a leader, I feel a responsibility to encourage others and to support individuals who want to make a difference. I am grateful for my family, my health, and my community. I am very proud of my two wonderful daughters, who both stand up to challenges and who dream big.

We believe we can shoot for the stars and continue to follow our dreams. If our journey leads us in unanticipated directions, so be it: we will take the chance to view things from a new perspective, and enjoy the ride along the way.

Founder and president of Sirius Financial Services in Ottawa, SUSAN ST AMAND (CLU, CH.F.C., TEP, FEA, ICD.D) is passionate about families. She specializes in continuity planning for family enterprises, co-creating strategies for value-based plans directed toward their desired future. Her strong technical skills and expert knowledge of financial instruments, governance, and strategy make her uniquely skilled.

THALIA KINGSFORD

THIS IS THE earliest picture I have of a very special car, my 1969 Morgan. Today, my Morgan lives in semi-retirement, in the garage located under my bedroom. As I tell it, it's "tucked safely under my bed."

This car has been a huge part of my life for fifty years, and the adventures we have shared are my story.

I have loved cars since childhood. Around the kitchen table, my siblings and I would compare our "dream cars": the exact make, model, year, and colour. When I was eighteen, I made the massive decision to change my dream car to a Morgan. Somehow, I convinced my boyfriend to buy one and, in 1969, when I was at the University of British Columbia, my dream car became our car. It was a huge part of my identity, and I couldn't separate it from my own concept of who I was. I made a yellow sundress to match it—I wish I could find that picture.

We got married in 1970, and, of course, the car was there. My brothers filled it with shaving cream and potato chips, which forced us to use a different car for a while—that, in turn, led to more issues, which led to my new husband losing his job. At that time I had a part-time job in a tough neighbourhood in East Vancouver. One day, while I was at work, the accelerator cable broke. I couldn't abandon the Morgan, so I used my pantyhose to create a hand throttle, and I drove it home anyway.

In 1971 we moved to the Alberta foothills and my husband became a ranch trainee. To make the move, I had to agree to sell "that silly car" so we could drive a truck. I sold the Morgan to my brother, keeping first right of refusal to buy it back. And, two years later, it was mine again. Age was taking its toll, but it happens I was also taking flying lessons, so I got the airplane mechanics (who could make any damaged plane airworthy) to restore it. I had started a successful farm and ranch real estate career, and that funded the work.

In 1986, the ranch and our own farm was sold and our life changed. To improve my inadequate investment knowledge, I enrolled in the Canadian Securities Course. Then, out of nowhere, came two unsolicited job offers. Our family moved to Calgary and I became a rookie broker. The strain of these changes became too much for our marriage, and I eventually left with my children, my cat, and the Morgan.

Through the years following my career grew, and, in 2002, I was accepted into the Advanced Management Program at Harvard Business School. I thought the Morgan would fit right in, so had it transported to Toronto. We (the Morgan and I), drove from there to Boston, through the gorgeous countryside of New England. That car became my refuge in moments when the program seemed overwhelming.

Today, the Morgan has a very special place in the hearts of my children and grandchildren. Whether they're taking it out for a drive or just sitting in it, they consider it a family treasure. My car is fifty years old this year, and every time I walk into the garage, it's like seeing an old friend. It still turns heads, and it will always be my "dream car."

THALIA KINGSFORD is VP and senior investment advisor at BMO Nesbitt Burns and team leader of Kingsford & Associates, an all-woman wealth management firm. As a founding member and current chair of the Calgary chapter of the International Women's Forum Canada, Kingsford empowers women to find their voice and build opportunities within the global business community. For over thirty years, Kingsford has opened doors for women with an unwavering commitment to female leadership.

JANET McKEAGE

MUSIC IS AT the core of my fearless nature. I was the youngest of four kids, and being raised in a military family meant I was often the new kid in town. I remember trying hard to fit in and desperately wanting to be accepted. Eventually, I began to see that when I sang, people listened.

The picture of me you'll see on the next page, taken when I was thirteen, captures that empowering feeling. I remember hearing news over the school intercom of auditions for a special fundraising show put on by the Royal Canadian Mounted Police for our local children's hospital. I told my mom about it, and when she called, she was told they had over three hundred kids auditioning—but they would squeeze me in.

I had never auditioned for anything like this before, but figured it was worth a try. I auditioned in front of eight judges, and two weeks later was told I had been chosen for the junior chorus. But I also learned that they wanted me back, with seven other girls, to audition for the solo role as Annie, singing "Tomorrow."

Not knowing the movie or the song, I nervously returned for my second audition. I was terrified, and prayed I wouldn't forget the words. This one was serious!

I won the part. Being a fearless girl at my auditions led to two incredible months preparing for six sold-out shows, with an audience of more than ten thousand people. There were media interviews, meeting the governor

general of Canada, and even singing for Princess Diana and Prince Charles—
and then, three years later, for Prince Edward.

After that, I went to a performing arts high school, and then on to earn
a bachelor of music in vocal performance at university. I felt I was truly
accepted, as I won many local and national competitions, and even per-
formed at the National Arts Centre as Kate Pinkerton in Puccini's *Madame
Butterfly* at the age of nineteen.

But this fearless girl had another life lesson to learn. I attended a master's
class given by Phyllis Curtin, a famous opera singer and teacher. For a master's class, each student prepares and sings a song, and has the opportunity to
be coached in front of peers, other teachers, and the general public. When my
turn came, I sang a very emotional Dvorak song, and what happened over the
next thirty minutes was one of the most incredible things I have ever experienced. I learned the power of opening up your soul and letting people in.

Funny, I wasn't aware of anyone in the room except Madame Curtin. I
hung on her every word, sang the full piece, and, at the end of my coach-
ing time, I looked up to see the whole room in tears. My professor simply
told me that I was to always sing, giving all of myself—as anything less was
robbing people of my gift. Opening myself up like this for all to see is being

Opening myself up like this for all to see is being completely fearless. I began to live my life with this new sense of openness.

completely fearless. I began to live my life with this new sense of openness, now less worried about fitting in and rather just being a fully authentic me.

That fearless girl has emerged many times since then. I made it through a final year recital when my biggest fans, mom and dad, could not be there because my dad was dying of cancer. I began a career in finance, for that fearless girl shockingly accepted the challenge of the Chartered Financial Analyst Program, armed only with a degree in music. It was also that fearless girl who risked again after a devastating stillbirth at thirty-six weeks pregnant.

It is that fearless girl who has pushed me out of my comfort zone and led me to a career that I love and have excelled at. I now use all the skills I honed as a singer to build trusted relationships with clients and to lead a top-performing team. Every prospect meeting is an audition. Every panel discussion or board presentation is a performance. I now channel that fearless girl to raise awareness and funds for causes that are important to me, to mentor young women, and to raise strong, fearless daughters. We all need to embrace and nurture our fearless girl. Without her, I don't know where I would be today.

JANET MCKEAGE is vice president and investment counsellor at RBC PH&N Investment Counsel. She provides comprehensive discretionary investment management for affluent individuals, their families, and their corporations, foundations, and endowment funds throughout Central and Eastern Canada. She joined RBC in 1991 and is a Chartered Financial Analyst and a certified Personal Financial Planner. She is also a member of the International Women's Forum, an ambassador for women's mental health, and actively involved with other local charities.

SONYA
SHOREY

FOR AS LONG as I can remember, I have dreamed of doing "something big." As a little girl, my definition of "something big" evolved daily. One day I would dream of being a famous actress, the next an astronaut or scientist, or then a doctor who saved lives. One of my greatest and most consistent influences was my mother, a beautiful, strong, and impactful leader in her own right. I loved her deeply, and admired the difference she made as a nurse, hospital administrator, and professor. She was everything I aspired to be. And, together with my father—an equally significant influence on my life and growth—she provided unwavering, unconditional love and the encouragement to boldly pursue any dream.

When I look at this picture of myself at age four, I see an ambitious little girl filled with hope, excitement, and (likely too much) energy, performing for her parents . . . sharing big plans for doing something great. Their love planted seeds of confidence that allowed me to dream big, fight fear, and believe I could do anything, right there in our living room. And when I ventured beyond the safety of our home and their loving arms, those gifts were needed. I have carried them with me, and called upon them, every single day for the past forty-five years.

From the moment I entered school, I set ambitious goals and worked diligently to pursue them, no matter how far-fetched they seemed, or what challenges they presented. And, as does everyone, I met bumps, unexpected twists, and disappointments. Among all of my successes and failures, however

they were defined, the love of my parents served as my rock. I knew, no matter what I achieved, I would always be successful in their eyes.

This foundation gave me the courage to fight fear, build resilience, and relentlessly and passionately pursue my dreams with everything I had. This included a formative early role at Nortel that completely changed my life, leadership positions I didn't believe I was fully qualified for, the launch of my own management consulting business, and many global opportunities. Whatever I achieve in this life, I attribute to the love of my parents—a legacy I strive to live and share with others every day. And I have been so privileged to collaborate with many visionary leaders and organizations changing our world for the better.

This foundation gave me the courage to fight fear, build resilience, and relentlessly and passionately pursue my dreams with everything I had.

This later photo of me was shot at Bayview Yards, a one-stop business acceleration shop and the home of Invest Ottawa, the lead economic development agency for our region. There is a part of my heart here. I am incredibly grateful for the opportunity to play a leadership role in the creation and evolution of the first entrepreneurial and innovation hub of its kind in my city. Together with many talented leaders, innovators, and companies, I help architect, develop, and drive groundbreaking initiatives that I genuinely believe will strengthen and revolutionize the country's economy.

In this photo, I see the ambition, passion, and dreams of my younger self manifesting in ways I hope will have long-term impact. I see deep love and admiration for my parents, and for those who are closest to me. And I see gratitude for all those who have believed in me, created opportunity, and contributed to my leadership journey. I will pay it forward for the rest of my life. And I will never stop striving to achieve "big" impact.

SONYA SHOREY, VP of strategy, marketing, and communications at Invest Ottawa and Bayview Yards, has twenty years of leadership experience with private, public, and non-profit technology organizations. She has led, authored, and/or significantly contributed to successful public funding proposals valued at more than $164 million (not including industry contributions) that fuel entrepreneurship, innovation, and economic growth.

NICOLE VERKINDT

THIS IS A photo my dad took of me in Florida. Apparently, we spent the afternoon sitting at a high-top bar. I was drinking a Shirley Temple, feeling as if I were in my twenties, and then I wandered off on my own. Completely fearless.

My dad found me walking around, strolling really, with my hands in my pockets so casual, looking off into space, as if it were completely normal for a kid to be doing that. The knitted horse sweater and Velcro shoes really added to the picture!

I love this photo of me, because I have always been one to wander, alone, feeling completely in control, daydreaming away. I wish I had the time to do it more often today!

NICOLE VERKINDT is the founder and CEO of OMX, a procurement platform specializing in driving socioeconomic returns. She serves on the board of the Canadian Commercial Corporation and the Canadian Chamber of Commerce, and is co-chair of the Business Council of Canada's Task Force on Economic Growth. In 2019, Verkindt was named Startup Canada's Woman Ambassador of the year. She is also a frequent commentator and columnist, and has appeared on *Next Gen Dragons' Den* and *The Pitch*.

SUSAN DELACOURT

NOT LONG BEFORE my sixtieth birthday, an old high school friend sent me an envelope of photos she'd found, dating back to the late 1970s. "Your first writing gig," she wrote about one of the old grainy pictures.

Exactly true. Long before I joined the university newspaper that would give me my entry into professional journalism, my friend's father employed me for a week at the end of each summer to write a daily newsletter for a hockey-referee school he ran in my hometown of Milton, Ontario.

While I have no recollection of breaking any big stories or even what I wrote during that first assignment, I recognize this young girl sitting earnestly at a typewriter, dreams of a writing career floating around her like the plume of smoke from the nearby ashtray.

The typewriters and the ashtray disappeared, but not the hope of making a career out of writing. Did I dream that one day I'd be interviewing prime ministers as a national political columnist? Probably not. When I thought about a future as a writer back then, I imagined myself as a novelist, living in New York or Europe, churning out bestselling fiction.

Back in the late 1970s, I was interested in politics, certainly. I sat in the TV room of that same friend's house in May of 1979 and watched, riveted, as the vote counts came in and Pierre Trudeau was tossed out of office. I wonder

what I would have thought if someone had told me that, in roughly forty years, I'd be interviewing Trudeau's son in a Montreal restaurant, for a front-page prime ministerial feature in the *Toronto Star*? Now that would make a good novel.

The path from that referee-school writing gig to national political journalism was far from a straight line. I had to learn a lot along the way, about my country and myself. With help from some strong mentors, I was coaxed out of that safe space behind the typewriter, to overcome the shyness of a young girl and learn how to put a tape recorder in front of a politician, or put myself in front of TV cameras or a radio microphone. I had to learn to write books—not novels, as I'd once dreamed, but stories about politics.

Each risk was scary, sometimes funny, especially in retrospect, but always worth it. One important thing I learned was to take the opportunities that are offered—whether it's a one-week gig at a referee school (even if you know nothing about hockey or refereeing) or a chance to write a book.

Each risk was scary, sometimes funny, especially in retrospect, but always worth it. One important thing I learned was to take the opportunities that are offered.

When I walked into that interview with Justin Trudeau in the winter of 2018, I was flustered. The cab driver got us lost along the way, and I couldn't find the list of questions I'd prepared in advance. Trudeau had to pick up the tape recorder I dropped when I went to shake his hand.

I thought to myself: "You've been doing this for nearly forty years and you're still that girl from Milton." Yes, I guess I am.

SUSAN DELACOURT is an Ottawa columnist and bureau chief with the *Star* who has been covering politics on Parliament Hill since the late 1980s. She is the author of four political books, and is a regular commentator on TV and radio.

A Special Dedication

BETTY.

I know her in many different ways. She's formidable. Fun. Fiery. Fit. Stylish. Whip-smart. And fabulous. Her mega-watt smile continues to dazzle everyone who comes in contact with her. She's kept me on my toes since the day I was born. She's a woman of great beauty and grace who can turn into a lioness on a moment's notice to protect her three girls.

I've learned so much from my mother. A competitor extraordinaire, she's never let me win on the tennis court—I have to work to beat her outright. And even when I do, she's ready to challenge me again. From her, I've learned to never quit, and to look for different solutions to any problem. We both run scenarios to anticipate potential issues.

"Why" is my favourite word. Ever. And as a young girl, I think I drove her mad with my daily barrage of questions. Naturally curious, I would ask away about whatever I observed, thought of, or didn't understand. The typical parent answer of "because" would never satisfy me. I needed to make sense of the world. I still do.

Betty McDonald taught me to approach life with a can-do attitude, a love of hard work, and joy in the simple things, like nature. She continues to inspire me daily with her fearless approach to living.

She's also the person who knows best the meaning of this mischievous look.

JANICE

Acknowledgements

I AM GRATEFUL TO the all-women dream team at Page Two Strategies for sharing their amazing talent with me to bring this beautiful book to life: Jesse Finkelstein for understanding my magic formula for the project, Gabrielle Narsted for her jugglery skills that kept it all on task and on time, Taysia Louie for her spellbinding design, and Melissa Edwards for her word wizardry. To Veronica, who encouraged me do the book, and to the Captain, who supported me throughout. The biggest thank-you goes to each of the phenomenal, fearless women who agreed to give me their powerful stories to share with the world. You'll never know how much it means to me.

About the Author

JANICE MCDONALD knows that small hinges swing big doors. As a global champion for women, she's been pushing for equity since 1992, when she completed her first graduate degree and wrote her thesis on women on boards in Canada. She is an award-winning entrepreneur, a four-time WXN Top 100 winner and 2016 WXN Hall of Fame inductee, a sought-after speaker, and the co-author of three ground-breaking studies on women entrepreneurs in Canada, released in 2016, 2018, and 2020. McDonald has a BA in communications, an MA in Canadian studies, certification in conflict resolution from CICR, her ICD.D designation, and an MFA. Women in Trade–Los Angeles awarded her Global Trade Ambassador for Canada in 2017, and in 2018 she received an Inspiring Fifty women in tech award. Her Fearless Women Podcast, which she launched on Women's Day 2019, shares many more incredible stories like the ones you have read in this book. You can find it at thefearless.shop or wherever favourite podcasts are found.